Smashing Balls

Golf, Opening Doors for Women

BY

Dr. Debra Pentz and Peggy Briggs, LPGA

Praise for Dr. Debra Pentz and Peggy Briggs, LPGA

Smashing Balls

"I wish that I had a book like this when I decided in my early forties to play golf, on a more regular/serious basis. I taught myself to golf, but not very well. In spite of my poor skill level, I joined a Business Ladies League. I was always in the last group with the other unskilled golfers. I think we had more fun than anyone else in the league, and in that group, I met a lady who is one of my dearest friends some 30 years later.

"Golf was very valuable in my banking career. It helped me succeed in a 'man's world.' The golf course was a great venue to establish relationships, both with clients and staff alike, and get business done more easily than in a board room.

"If you haven't been compelled to get into golf yet, you really need to read this! Dr. Debra Pentz will give you a dozen life reasons why you should take up game and what you're missing out on and Peggy Briggs, LPGA will be your personal GPS on how to get started. You'll laugh, reflect, gain confidence and get inspired!"

—Char Carson

Former RE/MAX Long Drive Competitor, LPGA Teaching Professional

Also by Dr. Debra Pentz and Peggy Briggs, LPGA

Smashing Balls – Quick Start Guide to Participate in a

Golf Tournament

Smashing Balls – The Instructors Manual

Social Media

Scan this QR code with your smartphone or simply

click it to visit my website, www.smashingballs.com:

Smashing Balls

Golf, Opening Doors for Women

by Dr. Debra Pentz and Peggy Briggs, LPGA

Published 2014 by Dr. Debra Pentz and Peggy Briggs, LPGA

any information provided herein and before beginning any exercise, weight loss, or health care program.

All rights reserved. No part of this publication may be reproduced or transmitted in any form or by any means, electronic or mechanical, including photocopying, recording, or by any information storage and retrieval system, without permission in writing from the publisher. All images are free to use or share, even commercially, according to Google at the time of publication unless otherwise noted. Thank you for respecting the hard work of the author(s) and everyone else involved.

To our golfing friends – past, present and future.

"Sex and golf are about the only two things that you can

enjoy without being good at them."

—Jimmy DeMaret

Getting the Most from This Book

YOU WILL NOT be a professional golfer when you are through with the instructions in this book. If you are willing to let your hair down, even just a little bit, you will have fun and learn to enjoy golf.

Part 1 presents situations were golf opens doors, in the workplace and other life situations.

Part 2 focuses on etiquette, the basic rules of golf and how to play the game. The instruction is designed for **beginners**. We assume that you haven't recently, if ever, done much physically. Our first order of business is to get you moving properly. Allow yourself to have fun with it. The lesson progressions are skill based, so you move on when you have accomplished certain tasks. Go at your own pace.

Contents

Praise for Dr. Debra Pentz and Peggy Briggs, LPGA

Also by Dr. Debra Pentz and Peggy Briggs, LPGA

Social Media

Getting the Most from This Book

Contents

PART ONE

Why Women Should Play Golf_   page 1

Introduction   page 2

Door #1: Golf and Business   page 15

Door #2: Relationships   page 37

Door #3: Health & Self-Improvement   page 63

PART TWO

How to Play GOLF

The Game Of Lifetime Friendships   page 87

Introduction   page 89

Level #1: Putting   page 104

Level #2: Chipping & Putting   page 122

Level #3: Pitching, Chipping, & Putting   page 136

Level #4: Full-Swing Preparation   page 143

Level #4: (Continued) Smashing the Ball with a Full Swing   page 165

Level #5: Play Modified Golf   page 179

Level #6: Adding Clubs   page 202

Level #7: Special Shots   page 205

Level #8: Golf, the Real Thing   page 210

Level #9: Opportunities for More Golf   page 213

Glossary   page 216

Appendix #1   page 220

Appendix #2   page 224

Appendix #3   page 232

Appendix #4   page 234

Appendix #5   page 236

About Dr. Debra Pentz and Peggy Briggs   page 237

Your Thoughts?   page 242

PART ONE

Why Women Should Play Golf

Introduction

From: Donna Willard

Sent: Sunday, November 11, 9:44 PM

To: Debra Pentz

Subject: Golf

My challenge: *I want to play golf, my family and friends want me to play golf, but I don't know how to get started. As much as everybody wants me to start, nobody steps up to help. I have a rough idea of what the process might be: buy* clubs, dress appropriately, and learn how to swing the club so I can hit the ball in the correct direction.

What I don't know are the answers to these questions:

Do I need to own my own clubs? If so, how do I purchase clubs? I need to know details such as: do they come in sizes or lengths, how many do I need, what should the price point be, and what about the bag to carry them in? Are all clubs and bags basically the same? If not, what should I look for?

What clothing is appropriate when golfing? Is the "dress code" the same at all courses? Are golf shoes required?

How do I learn to golf? Do I need to take a lesson? If I should take a lesson, what should I look for? Can my friends teach me? Can I teach myself?

When do I know if I'm good enough to golf with my

friends who have been golfing for a while? Are there rules for how good you need to be before you golf on a course?

Before golfing with friends, how do I go about playing at a golf course? *Are all courses the same skill level? How much does it cost? How do I know the hours? Can I just show up? Can I golf alone? Do I always need to get a golf cart or can I walk the course?*

What happens if I'm on the course, and I need to go to the restroom?

Do you always need to golf 9 or 18 holes?

Is there only one way to keep score? Do you always keep score?

Is there a rule book? Is there only one rule book?

Please help!

~

DONNA IS MY younger sister, so I knew I needed to help her and thousands of other women who want to golf and don't know where to begin. Donna's email to me was a major influence that inspired me to write this book

First, I thought—I can teach her. Then I remembered when I tried to teach her to play tennis. I was 16 and Donna was 8 years old. I had only recently learned to play tennis, because I had a driver's license and could drive to the courts. The nearest tennis courts were three miles away from our country home.

Tennis requires a playing partner, which was not always easy to come by. My sister, even though younger, was athletic, and she was always around. Our mom and dad worked, and I took her everywhere with me, so she was a good candidate to be a tennis-playing partner. However, our first session on the tennis court didn't go well. If fact, after only 15 minutes, she threw her racquet at me and walked home—all three miles! The thought of a golf club flying at me caused me to consider other alternatives.

Second, I thought—get a book from the library, or buy her a book on beginner golf. I didn't find much. What I did find was that most golf instruction books are written by famous players and instructors in the golf industry. Most of them are "golf babies"—they have been playing golf as long as they can remember. For these people, holding a golf club is as comfortable as holding a toothbrush. Their books are good for people who already understand the basics of golf. However, the books don't apply to learning golf as an adult.

Third, I thought—what about my own experience? I "learned" how golf **opened doors** in the business world, in my relationships, meeting new friends, and with support systems. Many people I worked with golfed.

One in particular, Sandy, took me under her wing and gave me a list of things I needed to buy. She even went shopping with me. Then we went to the driving range, moved up to a real golf course (a short one designed for beginners), then to a real golf course. (I'll tell you more about how to find these facilities and how you know when you are ready to progress to the next level.)

When I decided to golf, taking lessons from a golf teaching professional didn't seem appropriate. In fact, I'm not sure that I knew the difference between a playing professional and a teaching professional. When Sandy and I went to the driving range, it seemed that the golf pro was teaching someone who already appeared to be a good golfer. I didn't have much money either, and though I didn't know how much lessons cost, I assumed it would be a lot. I knew so little—but you don't know, what you don't know.

I'm not sure what I would have done without Sandy. Once I started playing, there were many people who helped me. If fact, many people still help me, even after golfing for more than 30 years. But what if Sandy hadn't been there to help me? It occurred to me that entry into the world of golf is haphazard, especially for adult women.

So, I decided a book should be written to provide instructions specifically for women to enter the game of golf, to play golf, and to enjoy the opportunities golf presents.

Why Specifically Women?

1. More women are in leadership and management positions in companies, or they own their own businesses. Golf can "open doors" in the business world, if you know what you are doing.

2. Women, who are now adults, typically didn't have opportunities when they were younger to play most sports available today, so movement patterns are important to learn first. Many traditional golf instructors and instruction manuals skip over this.

3. Women are built different from men—our upper body is not as strong, so we need to capitalize on efficiency and use our hips and legs to generate power (if you have a big rear end, it's an advantage in golf!). Of course, another

difference is that we have larger breasts. If you are small-chested, it's no big deal when it comes to golf. However if you are buxomly, you need to know how to golf around your chest.

4. Women learn differently than men. Women like learning in social settings and are typically more coachable.

5. Women think they need to know how to play before they venture onto a golf course. They might be more timid about entering what has traditionally been a man's turf.

Women deserve their own instruction, geared toward their uniqueness.

Golf has truly enriched my life, and this book will help you understand how golf can open doors in your life in various ways.

The technical side of golf is not my expertise, so I sought

the help of my friend, Peggy Briggs, Ladies Professional Golf Association (LPGA), who is passionate about sharing the game of golf and its benefits to women—especially women just beginning to explore the possibilities of golf.

Like me, Peggy learned to play golf as an adult. Both of us enjoyed participating in sports as girls and young women, but in the time period when we grew up, golf was for rich kids and we did not fit that category.

Some still consider golf a sport for the rich. I guess it depends on your definition of rich. Thanks to professional golfers Arnold Palmer and Lee Trevino, golf moved from the hoity-toity country club crowd to the general public. Maybe it is a section of the general public, but perhaps that's one of the reasons you are attracted to golf—it is still a bit of a status symbol. Golf is available to a wide range of people from all walks of life.

This book is written for the following people:

The Novice

If you have never tried golf before, congratulations! You don't have to unlearn anything; with *Smashing Balls* you can immerse yourself in the experience without any preconceived notions.

The Teacher and Friend

If you are an amateur trying to help a friend learn the game, give *Smashing Balls* a try. Participate actively with your "student" and have some fun doing it. Resist the temptation to teach as you were taught. Going to the driving range to attempt to hit balls is not typically productive or fun. If your student is athletic, you might get away by starting this way. I liken this to enrolling in a martial-arts class and being asked to chop through a board in your first class. There will be that rare person who can do it, but fundamental instruction is always a good idea.

The Golf-Teaching Professional

If you are a golf-teaching professional, you might have doubts about trying something different. You might even call us crazy. However, physicist Albert Einstein's definition of insanity is doing the same thing over and over again and expecting different results.

How many times have you repeatedly given the same golf lesson and the golfer just doesn't improve? Do your beginning students fall in love with golf? Do you really

13

know how to deal with a true beginner, especially if she is an adult female without a clue about golf?

I expect that you will be pleasantly surprised how quickly students will progress using the *Smashing Balls* methodology. Don't be left behind using the same old methods. *Smashing Balls* jazzes up golf lessons, which increases interest and retention of the new golfer.

For everyone who reads this book, it is our sincere hope is that you will fall in love with golf at some level, and find golf to be a worthy companion that teaches you valuable lessons, enriches your life, and opens doors for you.

I'll be honest with you, I think it would have been easier and less painful to donate a kidney to my sister than to write this book, so I sincerely hope you enjoy it, find it helpful, and share it with your friends.

Door #1: Golf and Business

"Once you have the business skills you need, learn to play

golf."

—Susan Battley

PsyD, PhD, Performance Consultant

Advice to entrepreneurs on how to grow their business

THERE WILL COME a day when you smash the golf ball effortlessly down the fairway. When you reflect on your effort, you find that you were focused, yet your head was clear. Some people describe it as "playing empty headed."

And no doubt on that same day, you will hit a lousy shot. When you examine your shot, you are likely to notice that there were distractions. Some were external, such as a car alarm going off, a playing partner jingling keys in a pocket, somebody sneezes, or a butterfly lands on your ball just as you are about to strike it. Some were internal like, too many swing thoughts, thinking about your to-do list, or wondering if your rear end looks too big in your new golf shorts. Your thoughts and abilities to control your mind are an important life skill, and golf can provide a forum to practice this skill.

If you choose to play golf and stick with it, it's a good indicator that you will be successful in many aspects of your life. Playing golf requires many of the same attributes that successful business people have—persistence, fortitude, grit, focus, willpower, resolve, spirit, good decision making, a positive attitude, and staying in the moment. Golf can help you exercise those skills while you get some exercise and enjoy the outdoors.

Does this mean that if you don't golf you are nobody? Of course not. But think for a minute about being a golfer. What image comes into your head? Athletic, tan, well dressed (okay sometimes golfers dress weird), and wealthy. Do all golfers fit those adjectives? Absolutely not, but most of us aspire to those attributes.

Golf has a magical power of eliciting emotion and passion from even the most stoic person. Even professional golfers who make great shots routinely still get excited and pump their fists when they hit a particularly fantastic shot.

Entrepreneur Oprah Winfrey said, "The defining characteristic of every successful person I have seen. They have passion." Golf helps tap into passion.

The Working Woman

I was an accountant, and I was amazed how golf transformed my career. I was responsible for compiling, reporting, and analyzing department expense budgets— pretty boring stuff. Most managers (usually men) in engineering and manufacturing really didn't like (actually they hated) the budgeting and accountability process. I tried to be supportive and offer as much help as I could to make the process easier for them, but I always had a sense that they considered me a pain.

But then it all changed, I joined the company golf league. I must warn you. You might not be welcomed with open arms to a company golf league. Sometimes the golf league is considered a "men's league." It created quite a stir when I signed up to play in the company golf league. I was surprised by the brouhaha. The president of the golf league, Jim, called me to his office. Jim was a little intimidating. He was the director of packaging and shipping and had the reputation of ruling with an iron fist. He also was known to be the best golfer in the league.

His voice was deep and serious, "So, I hear you signed up for the golf league?"

"Yes, I started playing golf a few years ago, and I just love it."

"You know the golf league has always been considered a men's league."

In my mind I was wondering which decade I had suddenly been transported to. It was the 1980s, for crying out loud. I gathered my jaw off the floor and replied, "No, I thought it was a company league."

"We have never had a woman play in the league. It raises

a lot of questions."

I didn't know what to say. What questions? I didn't think it was a big deal. Obviously, it was to some of the men.

Jim seemed a bit sheepish as he formulated his next statement. "You know some of the guys are worried about what their wives will say."

There was an awkward silence. I was trying to contain my laughter. He was trying to not be embarrassed.

He explained, "The guys think of it as a guy's night out. Golf starts at 4:00, we're done about 6:00, and then we go to the bar for food and drinks for a few hours. Some of the wives might object if there is a woman in the mix."

I couldn't contain myself any longer. I laughed out loud. "Look, Jim, I really didn't sign up for the league to cause a problem. I simply want to play golf. If I am not welcome at the grill after golf, I will go home or somewhere else."

I wondered what the next issue would be. Apparently there were no more points to discuss. Jim said he would take my request to play in the league under advisement and get back to me. I was dismissed.

The next day I was summoned again to Jim's office. His posture was a little more relaxed. "I reviewed the bylaws of the golf league, and there is nothing that prohibits women from participating, so you're in. Those fellows who are henpecked are just going to have to deal with it. They have bigger problems than having a woman join the golf league." Now, I knew Jim was on my side. He loved golf, and wanted to include anyone who was enthusiastic about the game.

The next year, three more women joined the group. After a few more years, it seemed normal that the golf league was co-ed. No one can imagine now that there was such a fuss when I signed up for the league that first time.

After I joined the golf league, the managers treated me totally different. They were more receptive. They still didn't like the budgeting process, but they would return my phone calls and respond to requests more expeditiously. Instead of avoiding eye contact in the hallways and cafeteria, they would strike up a conversation. Usually it would start with— "How's your golf game?" or "How are you hitting them?"

That was more than 30 years ago, and things have changed, but not quickly enough. It wasn't until 2012 that Augusta National Golf Course invited two women into its membership—former Secretary of State Condoleezza Rice and South Carolina financier Darla Moore. Augusta National is an exclusive private golf club, which is the home of "The Masters Golf Tournament."

Playing golf and participating in company leagues and tournaments can be an effective way to open doors into the good ol' boys' network.

You Want a Promotion?—Golf

Lorri is one of the smartest people I know. She has a master of business administration (MBA) degree from the Walter Cronkite School of Journalism, and she hosts a radio show. In one of her past job experiences, she noticed that many of her peers were getting promotions.

She asked her boss, "What do I need to do to get a promotion?"

His answer was short and not so sweet, "Learn to play golf."

You might find his response offensive, and the criteria for a promotion unfair, even ridiculous. Certainly job competence should be criteria for promotion, but if it's a close call between a golfer and a non-golfer, the golfer will get the promotion in a company that has a golf culture and where the leaders play golf.

A Captive Audience—Quality Networking

The typical round of golf takes four to five hours to complete. There aren't many socially acceptable ways that a woman can spend that much time with male clients, coworkers, and bosses. Little of that time is spent actually hitting the ball. Typically there is a lot of time to interact with the people you are playing with. The interaction is not always verbal—your behavior speaks loudly when you react to how a poorly struck shot is handled, or how you approach a tough shot, such as being behind trees. Do you risk hitting the ball through the trees, or do you punch the ball safely into the fairway? Do you calm yourself, take a deep breath, and make the shot, or do you choke?

Golf is a great way for people to get to know one another. People tend to do business with people who they know and like. Golf is also a great filter. It can reveal and amplify behaviors not apparent in other business meetings or brief encounters. It helps you know who you like and who behaves in a way you do not like. Golf can help screen out dishonest people. Be observant, and you will learn much. Be aware, you are also under surveillance.

Business deals happen on the golf course and in the clubhouse after golf. Always be aware of the other players' demeanor. If they are totally into their game, they may not like to talk much on the golf course. You should never allow chatting to slow down the pace of play. **Make sure to study the etiquette guidelines. Good golfers will put up with a bad golfer who is fun to be around and who also understands etiquette, some basic rules, and the pace of play.**

Golf can be a great networking tool for working women, especially if you are in a leadership position in a company, an owner of a business or you are in marketing and sales.

Golf—You Can Play with Professionals, Celebrities and Influential People

Influential people play golf. For example, 15 of the last 18 US presidents have played golf. That goes back to William Taft, who served as president 1909–1913. Rumor has it that other presidents before Taft, such as Theodore Roosevelt, also played golf. They kept it secret, because golf was considered a rich man's game, therefore it might hurt their image among the electorate.

Recently a White House spokesman said that while politics, and in particular negotiations, on the federal budget would be a subtext to the day's round (of golf), detailed on-course talks were unlikely. But, he added: "Spending a number of hours together in that kind of environment can only help improve the chances of bipartisan cooperation. It certainly can't hurt, unless someone wins really big."

Presidents William Clinton, George W. Bush, his father George H. W. Bush, Gerald Ford, Richard Nixon, and John F Kennedy (reputedly the best White House golfer), all played the game regularly. Mr. Clinton even once conceived a free trade deal with Singapore during a floodlit, post-midnight round of golf in Brunei with the city-state's prime minister.

You might not have an opportunity to play with the president of the United States, but once you can make contact with the ball, you might have the opportunity to play with golf professionals or famous, rich, and influential people.

For example, rock singer Alice Cooper occasionally plays at Las Sendas Golf Course in Mesa, Arizona. It's a course that is open to the public. Friends who play at Las Sendas have had the pleasure of meeting Cooper and say that he is a good golfer and a genuinely nice fellow.

Playing with a Golf Professional and Supporting Charities

If you are just learning golf, this might sound like it's pretty far-fetched. I can assure you that you can be ready for this opportunity in just a few months. Here's how it works. Most professional golf tournaments have a pro-am (abbreviation for professional-amateur) where a golf professional will play with four amateurs. This occurs before the real tournament starts. It usually costs more than an average round of golf, but there is typically a charity that is the event benefactor. The PGA and LPGA raise millions of dollars for multiple charities and scholarships. To learn more, check out www.together.pgatour.com and www.lpgafoundation.org. Sometimes pro-am events are strictly fundraisers, and there is no tournament that follows.

One thing you should know about a pro-am is that the format is typically a **scramble**, which means that everyone hits the ball. Then you choose the best shot and everyone hits from there. It's a great way to play, especially when you are first starting out. It takes a lot of the pressure off everyone, except the pro.

Can you imagine getting to play with a professional in any other sport—baseball, basketball, football, soccer, volleyball, boxing, or tennis? If you managed to not pass out from overexertion (basketball or soccer), or suffer an injury (football or boxing), or be totally frustrated by a ball whizzing by you at 100 plus miles per hour (baseball, volleyball, or tennis)—you might chalk it up to I did it, but what's the chance that you will do it again?

This advice bears repeating—**Good golfers will put up with a bad golfer who is fun to be around, and who also understands etiquette, some basic rules, and the pace of play.**

The following is a true story. If you are a beginner, you might not understand all the lingo yet. Be patient, we will get to it. If you are a friend helping to teach someone or if you are a golf professional, this story demonstrates how golfers make assumptions about non-golfers.

Jan was a successful businesswoman in a man's world—auto collision repair. When she and her husband started the business, they both did everything, from the hands-on repair to the administrative tasks of billing customers and collections. As the business grew, they hired mechanics and auto-body repairmen.

Jan's role in the company shifted more toward administration, hiring, firing, and dealing with insurance companies. She was proficient and soon was presenting seminars to other auto-body shops. Marketing was part of her duties as a co-owner. One of the networking groups that she participated in was Business Networking International (BNI). BNI held an annual golf tournament to raise money for a scholarship for the Arizona State University entrepreneur program.

One of her associates in the group, Hank, begged her to participate. He presented logical reasons—fun, extended networking, a day out of the office, great food and beverages after golf, et cetera. He was quite enthusiastic.

Hank explained, "The format is beginner friendly. It's a scramble."

"A scramble? Are we talking about eggs or golf?" Jan was hoping her ignorance would stop Hank from pestering her to play.

Hank was such a good-natured fellow. That is one of the reasons Jan even considered participating. He chuckled and explained, "A four-person scramble means that everyone hits their balls and then choose the best shot. Everyone then takes their ball to that spot and hits from there. So if you have a really bad shot, chances are that you won't have to play your ball.

In a moment of weakness she agreed. "Okay, so what do I need?"

"Just wear comfortable shoes." Hank was teasing her a bit, because one of her trademarks was stiletto heels. Jan was only 5 feet 2 inches and liked to look people in the eye when she was talking to them.

The day of the tournament arrived. Jan got out of her blue Honda SUV. She started to walk toward the clubhouse in her comfortable shoes.

Hank came trotting out to greet her. "Hey there, glad you are here. Can I help you with your clubs?"

Jan felt a knot form in her stomach. "What clubs? You just said I needed comfortable shoes. You mean I need clubs? I paid a hundred bucks and I have to supply my own equipment? Isn't this like bowling where they supply the equipment if you don't have your own?"

Hank, ever the diplomat, said, "No problem, I'm sure we can borrow a set of clubs from the pro shop." Sure enough, they did borrow some clubs and Hank donated some golf balls for Jan to use.

Hank realized he was truly dealing with a total beginner. He suggested that they go to the driving range for a quick lesson. The lesson was simple. Watch the ball and swing hard. In a matter of 15 minutes, Jan was connecting with about every other shot.

Then it was time to tee off. They drove up to the blue tee boxes. Two of the three guys Jan was playing with teed off. Then they drove up to the white tee boxes. The third guy teed off.

Hank could see that Jan was wondering why different tee boxes were being used. He gave her a quick explanation about handicaps and that higher handicapped player played from the forward tee boxes. She would play from the red tee boxes. All that she understood was that she got to play from the red tee boxes. There was way too much to think about, to try to understand handicapping right now.

She couldn't put it off any longer. The guys had all hit pretty good shots, so the pressure should have been minimal. However, it was her first time on a golf course. She gathered her courage, and thought about the quick lesson she had recently received. Watch the ball and swing hard.

Jan did both of those things and smashed the ball. She was so excited. Hank was probably more excited and relieved than Jan. He asked her where the ball went.

"You said all I needed to do was watch the ball and swing hard. I have to watch where it goes too?"

Hank started to realize how much of his golfing knowledge he took for granted.

At the end of the day, the entire team had enjoyed themselves and had a lot of great stories to take away from the event.

Learning Points from This Story:

1. You should have your own equipment. You can also borrow clubs from the pro shop. Sometimes there is a rental fee for equipment. It's a good idea to call them first if you are going to do this.

2. Wear comfortable shoes.

3. Watch the ball, especially after you hit it.

4. There are different tee boxes that players of different skill levels start from.

5. A scramble format in golf has nothing to do with eggs. Each player hits the ball, then everyone goes to the best shot, and hits from there.

6. Have fun

Door #2: Relationships

One of the origins of the word "golf" is alleged to be—

Gentleman Only, Ladies Forbidden.

Today we have new words that fit the spirit of golf—Game

of Lifetime Friendships

WOMEN ESPECIALLY TREASURE friendships. If you're a career woman without a family, it's likely that your friendships are forged at work. Golf can be a great way to deepen those friendships. It can also be a great way to expand your horizons. The game and the competition are attractions for both sexes. For women, the relationships are important.

The Golf Course Is a Great Place to Meet Men

A woman I know, Sarah, expressed a sudden interest in golf. I knew she was considering retiring, so I thought maybe that was the trigger.

I asked, "Have you ever played golf?"

"No."

"Have you played any other sports?"

"I played some basketball in high school, but that was a long time ago. I think basketball was the only sport we had."

"So why do you want to learn to play golf?"

Sarah blushed and rolled her eyes. "Well, I met this man

on Match.com, and he is a golf fanatic."

Ah ha, the great motivators—love, passion, and excitement. Let's face it, as we age the ratio of men to women declines. So if you are interested in male companionship, it only makes sense to go where the men are. More men play golf than women, so the odds are better than other activities. So if you are a woman looking for a man, learn to golf. Dancing is more popular with women. If you are a man looking for a woman, learn to dance. The American Singles Golf Association is a great organization to meet people. There are chapters all over the country. You can find out more at www.singlesgolf.com.

Golf is a good filter of character. If the guy has a bad temper and throws clubs on the golf course, he is not a keeper, unless you like ill-tempered men. If he cheats, or can't count strokes on the golf course, steer clear. Either he is a dimwit or dishonest or both.

Golf Transcends Age and Gender (A Socially Acceptable Way to Become a Cougar)

I am an older woman (that was really hard to write) approaching sixty. I am not a cougar, however, if I was, I can see how golf might be used as a tool to meet young men in a socially acceptable setting. I have two good friends who happen to be young men. Our friendship is solely the result of our mutual love of golf.

One young man is a 21-year-old banker and works at the branch where I do business. The other is an industrious young man who has his own business and takes care of my air conditioning equipment. Both are avid golfers. In each case, I invited them to play at my club, Red Mountain Ranch. They graciously accepted, and we had a marvelous time.

Of course, after golf we had food and drinks and watched some golf on TV at the clubhouse. Perhaps the best part of the day occurred when my friend stopped by the table where I was having lunch with these young men and asked, "Is this your son?"

I responded, "No, these are my friends, Andy and Pete."

Then, I make introductions as the young men shake hands with my friend, I can see the questions forming in my friend's mind—"I wonder if she is a cougar? Darn, if I weren't married, I think I'd like to be a cougar."

I love golfing with my girlfriends, who are roughly the same age as me, but it's also great to play with others. It's especially fun to be the object of gossip where your friends consider you capable of "robbing the cradle." What other sport gives you the opportunity to engage and compete with young men who could be your son or grandson?

The Golf Course Is a Great Place to Meet Women

According to journalist Steve Sailer, the LPGA Nabisco major championship, formerly known as the "Dinah Shore," is one of the more interesting social phenomena around. According to Eliza Atwater of LesbiaNation.com, the tournament is a "lesbian lovefest." Planet Out calls it "the world's largest lesbian circuit party." Tourism promoters say it attracts 15,000 to 20,000 lesbians from across the country to the Palm Springs area each spring.

For many of the same reasons that the golf course is a great place to meet men, it is also a great place to meet fantastic women. Eliza was introduced to many of her best friends through golf. Eliza and her friends go on golfing vacations all over the United States, Canada, and to other great places, such as Australia. She says, "Sometimes we even invite the guys."

The Social Butterfly

If you golf, you can be part of many social events. Many conversations on the course lead to other functions, such as birthday parties, weddings, book clubs, dinner and lunch invitations, cocktail parties, bridge club, book club, wine tasting, and hiking—you get the idea. Even if you decide you don't want to play golf, you can still be involved. Golf tournaments need volunteers for registration and organization. There are unlimited possibilities for networking, social interaction, and developing lasting friendships.

Golf Provides Deeper Insight into Others

At Red Mountain Ranch, where I golf, there is an active women's league—more than 100 members. One of those members is Helen, a seventy-something widow who is an avid golfer. She goes to the fitness center and can often be seen walking to stay in shape. She has a sweet Southern drawl and wouldn't say "poop" if she had a mouth full. After golf on a Tuesday morning, we were enjoying lunch and chatting about this and that. Somehow the conversation drifted toward nudity.

Helen became animated and remarked, "My neighbor must be a nudist—he is always swimming or using the hot tub buck naked."

Of course we needed more details. Lois asked, "Which house does this guy live in?"

Helen hesitated for just a second, "The fifth house from the tee box on the right of the fairway."

There was a moment of silence as everyone determined the location and the identity of the resident.

Lois was the first to verify her suspicion, "Helen, isn't that house all of the way across the fairway from where you live?"

Helen huffed, "Yes, but I can see him clearly with my binoculars!"

If you had told me that sweet little Helen was a voyeur,

I just wouldn't have believed it. Of course, Helen isn't her real name. What is discussed at ladies golf league is strictly confidential. What happens in the ladies golf league, stays in the ladies golf league.

A Support System

Without a doubt, golf is one of the greatest games in the world—if not the greatest. However, it has become apparent to me that golf is much more than a game. In July 2012 my dad died. The support and caring through social media, cards, phone calls, face-to-face words of encouragement and hugs were primarily from my golfing buddies. It occurred to me that golf is much, much more than a great game. It is a social network and priceless support system..

The members of my golfing community are mostly baby

boomers, so we have splendid life experiences to share from the elation of the birth of grandchildren to the sadness and sorrow of the death of loved ones and friends.

It's a time of change for many of us and we should recognize that **it is our time**. Retirement, the death of a spouse, the illness or death of parents and close relatives, divorce, and the empty nest are just a few of the ups and downs we must take in stride. Golf and our golfing buddies help us embrace and cope with change.

After Divorce, Golf Helps You Keep Swinging

"The Swing's the Thing" from *Chicken Soup for the Woman Golfer's Soul* tells the story of **Mary Murphy Fox:**

In the early 1980's, I developed an interest in the

challenging game of golf. One of my inheritances from my divorce settlement was a set of junior boy's golf clubs that had been collecting dust in the basement. Everything else I got had a payment book with it, including a mortgage with twenty-five years to pay.

I had been told it is pretty expensive to play golf, so I wasn't sure my budget could allow it. Hiring a babysitter only to hit balls into the woods on bad shots would be like losing dollar bills.

Neighbors and friends encouraged me to try the game. I could hear the voice of my college gym teacher during the mandatory golf lessons, "You have a natural swing." My father was an avid golfer as well. So with reliable babysitters in place and my cleaned-up set of golf clubs from the basement, I started to play once a week with a group of fellow

48

teachers. We were all beginners, so it wasn't very competitive. I enjoyed the game the very first time and was totally inspired by the beautiful walk with nature, taking the time to admire the sun, the sky, the mountains and the lakes. Doing this with companionship of three other women was remarkable and refreshing.

Of course, I struggled with the swing and losing balls, but that was overcome by the level of enjoyment.

Golf is full of lessons if one pays attention. I feel renewed in some way each time I play. Waiting on the first tee to start the game teaches me patience that good things are worth waiting for. It's so different than waiting in line to pay that grocery bill, which is always higher than you expected. Losing a ball in the woods teaches one how to deal with disappointment.

49

Golfers take five minutes allowed to look for a ball, then drop a new ball and get over it and move on. What a good principle to apply to life when you are thrown off course.

Mentally, golf provides the same level of concentration as yoga, but in an entirely different way. A round of golf is about you and your connection to yourself, the little white ball, the club, the swing, and the topography and the turf of the golf course.

Golf gives one the courage to play with better players and to take risks, resulting in one's becoming a better player and possibly a better person. The competition helps us get out of those old, negative, comfortable ruts that have become our friends instead of our enemies.

The little white ball is a symbol of life. Sometimes it goes smoothly in the right direction, and other times it gets off to a bad start, goes in the wrong direction, and may even get lost. But the game goes on, just like our lives. The freedom to swing the club on the tee is exhilarating because it is as if you are saying, "Look out, world, here I come."

So after the divorce came the swing that gave me the strength to keep swinging. This game of pleasure and companionship changes my attitude, my friendships, my energy level, and my daily outlook at spirituality both on and off the course.

Golf will enrich your life until the day you die. I'm confident that if you are a golfer, you will not die alone. How can I make this claim? You rarely golf alone, and you are bound to develop friendships. For women, camaraderie is the number one reason to play golf. Friendships that are forged on the golf course transcend to other areas of our lives, even until the day we die.

Golf leads to nights out with the girls—sometimes even vacations. Here's a story that illustrates what I'm talking about:

When Allison invited us to her winter pad for a long weekend of golf, my first reaction was, "Are you crazy! Just a bunch of girls? No guys? No hand-holding strolls on a moonlit beach? No dancing under the stars?" I could not imagine it. To me, a tropical getaway spelled romance. Love stuff.

But not wanting to be left out of something that, who knows, might actually turn out to be a good thing. I couldn't say no. And let's face it, these were my friends, my lunch group, my weekly Thursday foursome. I knew I could be replaced, and there was no way that I wanted to be left out and then have to hear them go on and on about their next outing.

I didn't want to listen to them rehashing the great golf, the dinners at the club, and the fantastic off-season bargains in the pro shop, that cute yellow golf shirt that was half price. I wanted to be part of it, to belong. So I packed a bag and, dragging my clubs in my black canvas travel bag with the tiny little wheels, headed to the airport with the girls.

And you guessed it. We had a great time. Played golf at three different courses, three days in a row; ate fried clams and calamari at a local fish place; laughed ourselves silly over stupid things, our unbridled giddiness no doubt nudged along by pitchers of margaritas: and stayed up late into the night playing vicious, competitive games of Taboo.

We took a couple of lessons at one of the clubs and actually got out to the courses early so we could practice. We played skins for ten cents a hole, and bet a dollar on closest to the hole on par threes. We were relaxed. Happy.

The next year, we couldn't wait to make a date to do it all over again. But we made a major mistake. We talked too much. Our men heard us wax poetic over the condition of the golf courses, the clubby bars. Oh, we were so smug. We even mentioned, barely mentioned, the hot lady pro at one of the courses. Super swing she had. Great clothes.

"Hey, sounds like a good time," said Allison's husband as we sat having dinner one night.

"Yeah," said Jimmy. "What do you say we join

you on the next trip? We'll have a ball."

"Ah, hmmm," we all sat quietly thinking.

"Good idea," I said. "But what about your annual Myrtle Beach outing with the guys?"

"What about it?" said Jimmy.

"Isn't that the last weekend in April?"

"That's the date."

"Well, that's a shame," Allison said (she was a quick study). "That's the same weekend we're going on our trip."

"That's right. Pity you won't be able to join us," I added wearing my best sad face while making a mental note to add our girlie golf trip to my calendar now that we had a firm date. Oh yeah.

—Katherine Dyson

The Thelma and Louise Effect

Doing crazy stuff with a partner or group is more fun; preferably with a group of women. This is especially true for golf. There is a comfort level and support when it's "just the girls" getting together to learn and play. There is also the accountability factor. If you are committed to meeting your friends to learn to play golf, it is more likely that you will show up. If you are doing it on your own, you might look out the window and see a few clouds. And you make excuses, such as maybe it will rain; I really should dust; it's the last day of that great sale.

The influence of partners and groups is powerful. Many organizations leverage this power, whether it is the weight loss industry, Alcoholics Anonymous, book clubs, or religious groups.

Our best efforts to stick to a plan always involve a partner, whether it is working out or writing a book. Having a partner or group to learn golf with, will help you stick with it and have more fun in the process.

Friends for Life

"Friends are people who help you be more yourself, more the person you are intended to be."

—Merle Shain

Golf is a lifetime sport, and your golfing girlfriends become your friends for life. Let me share a story about two golfing friends.

Barb learned to play golf when she started to work at a manufacturing company in York, Pennsylvania. She had moved from a small village in rural Pennsylvania to get a job in her chosen field of accounting. Her job demanded a lot of work hours, and her co-workers quickly became her family.

Her favorite co-workers had two things in common. They loved to party and to play golf. Her friend, Linda, offered to "show her the ropes" on the golf course. Linda had been playing golf for about ten years and was a great ambassador of the game. Linda had some old golf clubs that she let Barb borrow. Barb took the initiative to find a driving range to learn how to hit the ball. Barb had played field hockey in college only a few years previously, so she made good contact with the ball from the start.

The women decided to go to a short, easy, nine-hole course after work on a Friday. Of course, drinks were planned, so regardless of the golf, it was going to be a good evening. Both Linda and Barb were nervous on the first tee. Barb had never played on a real golf course. There were buildings and houses that could sustain damage from an errant shot. Scarier yet, there were people in harm's way.

Barb had been reading about golf etiquette and had learned to shout "fore," if a ball was going toward someone. She prayed that she wouldn't need to do this. Linda was nervous for Barb. She remembered her first outing to a golf course with her fiancé. She shot a 126, missed the ball completely several times, and lost four balls.

Linda was hopeful that Barb would like golf, or at least not humiliate herself, but it turned out that there was little to worry about. Barb was a natural. She only needed help with etiquette, such as how to mark your ball on the green. At the end of nine holes, Barb had a 48 and Linda had a 49. A lifelong friendly competition had begun.

They played once a week, weather permitting, for the next five years. The clubhouse bar and grill and the 19th hole was always part of the routine. Linda would always have a gin and tonic and Barb a beer.

The weekly competitions between Barb and Linda ended when Linda's mom, who was in her eighties, began to develop dementia or Alzheimer's disease. Nobody could seem to pin down the diagnosis. Linda decided she needed to move to Charleston, South Carolina, to take care of her mother. Linda fell in love with Charleston, discovered some great golf courses, and decided to move there permanently. Every few years, Barb would visit Linda and the competition was on again, along with the 19th-hole gin-and-tonic and beer ritual.

For the first several years, Linda's mom was physically well enough to play golf. She just needed to be reminded which direction to hit the ball. Linda noticed that even though her mother couldn't hit the ball as far, her short shots around the green were better than ever. Linda had always heard athletes talk about being in the zone, or playing empty headed. She knew when she hit her best shots that she didn't have a thought in her head. Perhaps that explained her mother's new found prowess around the green.

When Linda's mother died, Barb flew to Charleston for the funeral. After the services, Barb and Linda played a round of golf. This time they brought a cooler with them. The cooler didn't contain any beverages—it held an urn. The cooler served as camouflage, because Linda didn't want to freak out the golf course employees. Throughout the round, ashes would be distributed at the prettiest places on the golf course. Linda's mother's only request was that none of her ashes come near a bunker (novices might call it a sand trap). She hated being in bunkers. The last thing she wanted was to spend eternity in a bunker!

After the round at the 19th hole, Barb and Linda made a promise to each other to spread the ashes of whoever departed this life first. Golf created a bond between Barb and Linda that lasted longer than a lifetime.

Golf Can Be a Support Group for Widows

The facts are that women live longer than men. Given that most men marry younger women, it becomes evident that there will be an abundance of widows after the men die. Women who golf have a built-in support system.

Loneliness can be emotionally difficult and can even lead to physical illness. If you are a golfer, you have the opportunity to be active and around people every day, if you choose.

Door #3: Health & Self-Improvement

The Retiree

Believe it or not, golf can actually prolong your life. A recent study conducted by the Karolinska Institute (Sweden) was published in the *Scandinavian Journal of Medicine and Science in Sports.*[1] Data was compiled from studying more

---

[1] B Farahmand, G. Broman, U. De Faire, D. Vagero, and A. Ahlbom, "Golf: A Game of Life and Death—Reduced Mortality in Swedish Golf Players," *Scandinavian Journal of Medicine and Science in Sports* 19, no. 3 (June 2009): 419–424.

than 300,000 Swedish golfers and the study found the death rate for golfers was 40 percent lower than for other people of the same gender, age, and socioeconomic status. This equates to a five-year increase in life expectancy for regular golfers. So you can avoid being one of those people who retires and immediately dies.

If you must wait until you retire to play golf, I understand. Golf does take a chunk of time that can be difficult to squeeze in when you have a full-time job. However, remember that 15 of the last 18 US presidents have taken the time to golf. When you finally find yourself with 40 or 50 extra hours during the week, there is no better way to fill it than with golf.

Golf Is an Empty-Nest Remedy

Think of those little round golf balls as eggs. The best part is that they do not hatch, and you are not responsible for taking care of another being. In fact, you can smash those little orbs down the fairway without any fear of being turned in for hurting someone!

When the kids finally leave the nest, it's a great time to take up golf. The grandkids might not show up for a few years. Even if they do, what better game than golf to share with your grandkids, nieces, and nephews? You probably won't to be running around playing soccer or basketball. In fact, the methods in this book can be used by kids. You might even be considered a cool grandma or aunt, if you take the time to help youngsters learn the greatest game in the world.

However, a word of warning—just as you need to

develop fundamental movement and sports skills, so do children. If you approach golf like most instructors, the kids will be bored and frustrated. They will learn to hate golf, and if you persist with "no-fun" lessons, they might even dislike you. Design your golf learning experience to be a fun endeavor. It's especially important when you introduce children to the game of golf, that it be fun!

If Not for Yourself, Play Golf for Others

Playing golf is good for the economy. If you play golf, it is more likely that you will retire earlier. This can open jobs for people who really need them—moms and dads with kids to feed and clothe. People who don't have a hobby, such as golf, just keep working away and are seemingly being productive. Your experience and dedication are admirable, but step aside, learn to PLAY golf, and give the younger generation a chance to be productive.

Moms and Grandmas

Golf is a great family activity. Certain sports, such as football, basketball, baseball, and soccer, don't lend themselves to the average mom playing with and competing with their kids. No matter what your age, you can play golf.

Many of the lessons in *Smashing Balls,* Part 2 (The How!!) of this book can be used with your kids and grandkids. Take the kids with you. The lessons are designed to be fast-moving and fun. Your kids will benefit from the movement skills that are developed through the lessons.

It's important that girls learn a sport. Sports teach kids to compete, confront insecurities, focus on the task at hand, and commit to doing their best. Those lessons aren't unique to sports. They apply in the boardroom, the classroom and life. Girls who play sports are three times less likely to get pregnant in their teenage years, 80 percent more likely to leave men that abuse them, and 50 percent more likely to go to college. (source – "An Incredible Journey" Lyn St. James – 7 time Indy 500 Driver)

The role of grandma has changed in the past fifty years.

The "with-it" grandmas are the ones who can go out and play with their grandkids, and golf is the perfect venue to do just that.

Golf—An Easy Way to Get Your Vitamin D

Every tissue in the body, including the brain, heart, muscles and immune system, has receptors for vitamin D, meaning that this nutrient is needed at proper levels for these tissues to function well.

Studies indicate that the effects of a vitamin D deficiency include an elevated risk of developing (and dying from) cancers of the colon, breast and prostate; high blood pressure and cardiovascular disease; osteoarthritis; and immune-system abnormalities that can result in infections and autoimmune disorders like multiple sclerosis, Type 1 diabetes and rheumatoid arthritis.

Most people in the modern world have lifestyles that prevent them from acquiring the levels of vitamin D that evolution intended us to have. The sun's ultraviolet-B rays absorbed through the skin are the body's main source of this nutrient. "As a species, we do not get as much sun exposure as we used to, and dietary sources of vitamin D are minimal," Dr. Edward Giovannucci, nutrition researcher at the Harvard School of Public Health, wrote in The Archives of Internal Medicine. . . .

Although more foods today are supplemented with vitamin D, experts say it is rarely possible to consume adequate amounts through foods. People in colder regions form their year's supply of natural vitamin D in summer, when ultraviolet-B rays are

70

most direct. But the less sun exposure, the darker a person's skin and the more sunscreen used, the less previtamin D is formed and the lower the serum levels of the vitamin.

—Jane E. Brody

New York Times, July 26, 2010

For more information on Vitamin D, refer to *The Vitamin D Solution* (Hudson Street Press, 2010), by Dr. Michael F. Holick (www.drholick.com) of Boston University.

Golf Provides Introspection

Many seekers go on pilgrimages and consult with gurus to find answers about the meaning of life and how they can become the best people they can be. Golf has some great life

71

lessons, if you choose to pay attention, and you don't have to go to the ends of the earth to learn the lessons. Golf can be revealing, when it comes to your character. You can use golf as a mirror to examine your strengths and weakness. Some people say that is what a soul mate should do. I'm pretty sure learning golf is easier and much less complicated than finding a soul mate.

"People think a soul mate is your perfect fit, and that's what everyone wants. But a true soul mate is a mirror, the person who shows you everything that is holding you back, the person who brings you to your own attention so you can change your life". —Elizabeth Gilbert

The Loner

There aren't many sports the average person can do alone. Most, such as basketball or volleyball, require a team of people. Tennis requires two people of the same relative skill level. It's not a good idea to go hiking alone. Walking, running, and biking are great, but golf is a better option for people to participate in as they age.

When I was going through a particularly difficult time in my life (divorce and the potential loss of my business), I found solace on the golf course in the late afternoon. The course was empty—I carried my bag and walked the course. As a walked, I noticed the rabbits and quail scurrying about.

My focus was on smashing the golf ball and watching it intently.

When playing golf alone, more attention is required. There are not extra sets of eyes watching the ball and gauging where it might have come to rest. However, alone I was treated to many fantastic sunsets. The golden light of the evening, that photographers appreciate, illuminated the golf course to accentuate its natural beauty. The golf course is like Mother Nature in an evening gown. It's an easy place to enter a meditative state and tap into your spirituality.

Bling Is the Thing

If you like bling, golf has lots of opportunities for expressing yourself. The clothing can be stylish, not to mention the golf bag, the shoes, and even the ball markers lend themselves to bling. Headcovers for your clubs can range from the ordinary and functional to the exotic. Some headcovers look like fancy puppets of stuffed animals. Here are a few innovative samples.

Walking—Burning Calories

Oprah Winfrey said, *The most important person in your life is yourself.* One way to take care of you is golf. Let's read more about that:

Golf is good for you. That's the conclusion of a study recently completed by an American sports scientist. But we didn't need a scientist to tell us that, did we? Golfers know that getting out on the course, swinging the club and—especially—walking is a bit more than just a leisurely stroll in the park. We already knew that golf requires coordination, concentration, and, yes, physical effort, to play successfully.

But it's always nice to have an expert verify those beliefs. Particularly when the study in question revealed some interesting and very specific conclusions about the value of golf as exercise, and also about the effects of different kinds of effort on the golfer's score.

The scientist who conducted the study is Neil Wolkodoff, who is the director of the Rose Center for Health and Sports Sciences in Denver, Colo.

According to the lengthy Associated Press article about the study's findings, Wolkodoff recruited eight amateurs, all men, with ages ranging from 26 to 61 and handicaps ranging from 2 to 17. The volunteers were fitted with various sensors and measuring equipment, and then each played the front nine of a hilly suburban Denver golf course several times over the course of the study period.

During these 9-hole outings, the golfers varied their means of transportation (walking, riding in a cart) and also their means of transporting the golf bag (on a golf cart, on their shoulders, on a push cart, on a caddie's shoulders).

Among the findings were these numbers (remember, the figures cited are for nine holes only):

Calories Burned

Walking: 721

Using push cart: 718

Using caddie: 613

Riding: 411

Miles Walked

Not riding in cart: 2.5

Riding in cart: 0.5

The study concludes that golfers who walk 36 holes a week will burn around 2,900 calories per week. The threshold of 2,500 calories burned in a week is an important one; according to the AP article, "studies have shown that those who burn

2,500 calories a week improve their overall health by lowering their risk of heart disease, diabetes and cancer."[2]

Why Should Kids Have All the Fun—Let's Play

Imagine walking down the street and hearing laughter and hollering coming from around the corner. You assume it is a group of kids playing. When you turn the corner you see adults, some of whom are blindfolded and being led around by other adults. Balls are flying through the air as the blindfolded people are trying to tag other blindfolded people. In the midst of it all you see that these people

---

[2] Brent Kelley, "Guess What? Golf Is Good for You," About.com Golf. Accessed June 21, 2014.

are clearly having fun.

What do you do on a regular basis for fun? When was the last time you went down a slide, played hide and go seek or a good game of whiffle ball? Many adults have the mindset that they are too old to play. There is actually strong evidence that this could not be further from the truth. Play may be the very thing that keeps you young and healthier. In fact, studies show that a life lived without play is at increased risk for stress related diseases, mental health issues, addiction and interpersonal violence.

According to the National Institute, play is the gateway to vitality. By its nature it is uniquely and intrinsically rewarding. It generates optimism, seeks out novelty, makes perseverance fun, leads to mastery, gives the immune system a bounce, fosters empathy and promotes a sense of belonging and community. Each of these play by-products are indices of personal health, and their shortage predicts impending health problems and personal fragility.

Play also enhances relationships. The National Institute for Play cites studies that indicate that play refreshes a long-term adult-adult relationship. Some of the hallmarks of its refreshing, oxygenating action are: humor, the enjoyment of novelty, the capacity to share a lighthearted sense of the world's ironies, the enjoyment of mutual storytelling, and the capacity to openly divulge imagination and fantasies.

Believe it or not, the adults who were seen playing blindfolded were actually working. This playfulness was part of a work activity. When finished, almost without exception, each person commented on how good it felt to play and how energized they felt. When they sat down to actually work on a project, many commented that they could feel the high level of energy in the room.

Just as children need play to help them de-stress, adults need play to help them be at their best when it comes to career, parenting, and marriage. Instead of looking at play as a waste of precious time, consider it a great investment in your wellbeing.[3]

Get Ready to PLAY

The methods we advocate involve play. You might be thinking that you are an old lady and way past the play stage.

[3] Julie Baumgardner, "The Importance of Play for Adults," First Things First website. Accessed June 21, 2014.

And you think that you will probably feel silly playing in public.

If these are your thoughts, let's go into more detail about why play is good for you at any age. As people age, they shouldn't really care about looking silly in public. If what they are doing makes them happy, is good for them, and takes them in the direction they want to go, who cares?

Play for all ages involves developing physical skills, in addition to dexterity and social skills. Golf doesn't always result in fun, but then neither does mountain climbing, where there is danger of frostbite and battling severe conditions. So, why do people do it? There is a keen sense of accomplishment. Just as hikers climb a mountain, the game of golf can lead you to a sense of achievement and improved self-esteem and confidence as you learn the physical and social skills associated with the game.

I recently had a chance to listen to the thoughts of Dr. Stuart Brown, as he spoke at a conference on the topic of "Play Is More than Fun." Brown is a psychiatrist and clinical researcher, who shared these thoughts about play:

"Nothing lights up the brain like play."

"When play is deprived, development is arrested."

"The opposite of play is not work, it's depression."

"We are designed to play through our whole lifetime."

"Play is important for our survival."

"Play has a biological place in our health—just like sleep and dreams"

"The basis of human trust is established through play signals that we tend to lose as adults."

These are important concepts to ponder as you learn more about yourself and the interactions you have with others. Consider the impact that golf has on all parts of your life—to enhance your physical, social, mental, and emotional well-being—and all while playing! It doesn't get much better than this, does it?

PART TWO

How to Play GOLF
The Game Of Lifetime Friendships

"Golf is deceptively simple and endlessly complicated. It satisfies the soul and frustrates the intellect. It is at the same time rewarding and maddening—it is without a doubt the greatest game mankind has ever invented."

—Arnold Palmer

Introduction

WELL, HERE WE go with the nitty-gritty of why you bought the book. How ***do*** you golf? We plan to take you through a journey that is best done with a friend or several friends.

You might wonder whether you need lessons from a golf professional. That depends entirely on you. Nearly 85 percent of golfers learned golf on their own, or with the help of a friend or relative. We're interested in giving you instructions to self-start your golfing adventure. If you decide to work with a golf pro, see Appendix 3—How to Select a Golf Teaching Professional.

Orientation

Watch golf on TV. How easy is that? You'll become familiar with terminology, etiquette, and see how different shots are made. Watch the ladies (LPGA) or the men (PGA). Observe their posture, what the shape of the golf swing looks like, and what they look like at the end of the golf swing. Find a full-length mirror and see if you can mimic their posture and their finish position. These will be things we will try to emulate.

Listen to the announcer's golf vocabulary (listen for words that are listed in the Glossary of this book).

Pay attention to the type of tournament that is being played. The most common is individual-stroke play, where every stroke is counted. There are other formats, and the announcer is likely to point out the type of match being played.

Notice—everyone is quiet and nobody moves when a golfer is about to play a shot. Players are careful to keep their shadows from distracting other players.

When players hit the first shot of each hole, they will put the ball on a tee between and slightly behind the tee markers that indicate the starting line for the hole. The club that a golfer uses to start the match is usually the longest and biggest club that a player carries—many times it is a driver.

Golf holes are different lengths and are assigned a par number. Par is the number of strokes a professional golfer is expected to take from start to finish. Short holes are par 3. A medium-length hole is par 4, and a long hole is par 5.

In addition to the driver, there are four other major club categories in a golfer's bag—fairway woods, hybrids, irons, and a putter. Clubs are different shapes and are used in different circumstances. Notice that the higher numbered clubs are meant to hit the ball for a shorter distance than the lower numbered clubs. For example an 8 iron will go a shorter distance than a 7 iron.

When golfers get to the green, the short-mowed area where the hole is, they will use a putter that has a flat surface to roll the ball along the ground. This action is called putting. Think of the hole as the finish line for each hole. Also notice when the ball reaches the green, players can "mark" the ball and pick it up, clean it, and replace it when it is their turn to play. This is normally the only time you can pick up your ball. There are exceptions, but they are beyond the scope of this introductory book.

Observe the order of play. The golfer farthest away from the hole plays first. Whoever has the lowest score goes first on the next hole.

On the green, players are careful to not step between an opponent's ball and the hole. The flagstick is removed when a player is putting on the green. If players are off the green, they can choose whether they want the flagstick in or out of the hole.

Notice that putters come in all different lengths, shapes, and sizes. Players hold the putter differently, and putting postures vary widely.

Here are some things to notice, but not replicate:

Professional golfers might take a lot of practice swings. Do not do this. Maximum practice swings—two or fewer.

Players take a long time to line up a putt. They are playing on more difficult courses, and they have a lot of money of the line. When you line up a putt, go with your first instinct.

Caddies are only used at professional golf events and exclusive golf clubs and resorts. You will carry your bag of clubs, use a pull cart, or drive a motorized cart. Pull carts and motorized carts are available for rent from the golf course.

After you have watched golf a few times, you will quickly become familiar with the jargon. So now you can talk the talk. We still have some work to do so that you can walk the walk.

Action Item

Take a putter or yard stick. Stand in front of a full-length mirror. Make a putting stroke, like you watched the pros do. The lower body stays still. The shoulders and arms move in a pendulum motion, and the wrists stay locked. Do this for about 5 to 10 minutes per day when you are first starting to play golf. It will make your transition to the practice green much smoother.

You have begun to intellectualize golf, but you are likely

to still have some basic questions. Let's answer a few of those before we go on.

Do I Need My Own Clubs?

Eventually you will need your own clubs, but let's keep it simple to start. Buy or borrow a putter and a seven iron. You are likely to find these at a thrift store, on Craigslist, or on golf discount websites, such as www.rockbottomgolf.com. There is a good chance that your first putter will not be the only putter you ever play with. While you are shopping, you will need a yardstick or alignment sticks for the practice drills. Alignment sticks can be purchased online, or you can simply purchase mailbox reflector sticks from your local hardware store for about $2.

What about a Driver?

Lots of advertising is directed toward the driver and hitting the ball long distances. Driving the ball from the tee area is important and fun, but putting is more important. For every shot from the teeing area, it is likely you will make two putts. Putting is really important!!! And the cool part—everyone can putt the ball, regardless of physical strength, age, or ability.

Recently Deb's mother, Gloria—age 76—who had never played golf, came to Arizona for a visit from the snowy East Coast. One evening they went to the practice putting green at Red Mountain Ranch Country Club. They practiced putting from various distances. Deb didn't give her too much instruction. Putting is simple. If the ball doesn't get to the hole, hit it a little harder next time. If it goes too far, ease up. Of course you need to pay attention to whether the ground between you and the hole is uphill, downhill, or side hill—right or left. Yes—golf helps you pay attention to your circumstances.

So Gloria, who had never touched a golf club before in her life, got rather engrossed in putting. What Deb thought might be a 15-minute exercise turned into a 45-minute practice. It might have lasted longer, but the sun was going down. So the final challenge was this—whoever gets the ball closer to the hole is excused from doing dishes for the evening. They decided on a distance about 20 feet from the hole. Deb putted first. Her putt rolled toward the hole, drifted slightly left, rimmed the cup, and ended about a foot away. Gloria focused intently as she struck the putt. Deb couldn't believe it—the ball was tracking directly toward the hole. The ball dived into the hole like a rabbit being chased by a coyote. So despite Deb's years of experience and single-digit handicap, she lost the putting contest. Deb decided they would go out for dinner—she hates doing dishes.

The moral of the story—anyone can learn to become a good putter with a little practice.

What Kind of Golf Balls?

The other basic thing you need is golf balls. A box usually contains a dozen balls. To start, you only need a few balls, so you can buy a "sleeve," which will contain three balls. Many times you can find used (sometimes called experienced) balls at thrift shops, flea markets, and sometimes in the pro shop. No need to get expensive golf balls to start. Expect to get three used balls for a dollar.

What to Wear?

It can vary, depending on the golf course, but you will always be safe with a collared shirt. Your shoes should be tennis shoes, golf shoes, or golf sandals. Bermuda-length shorts, cropped pants, or long pants are the best choice for pants. Some golf courses forbid jeans and many will state the dress code on their websites. A hat and sunglasses are also advisable.

Getting to the Golf Course?

Deb's mother had the luxury of having someone take her to the golf course practice area. In case you are going it alone, here's what you need to know about getting to the golf course.

You might have a choice of golf courses, if you live in a metropolitan area. So how do you choose? Ask friends or relatives for a recommendation. Some golf courses are private or semi-private, so those are off limits for practice for now. Just make sure that the golf course has a practice facility. You can find that information online. If you go to a golf course where you don't feel welcome, find another, if you have that option.

When you drive into the golf course or driving-range parking lot, there might be an area that is labeled "bag drop." This will be a place where you can take your clubs out of your car and then park your car. Sometimes an employee will pick up your clubs and take them to the golf shop area. He or she might ask if you are playing or practicing. You will be starting with practice.

For your first session, you will only need a putter, so it is not necessary for you to drop off your clubs at the bag drop. After you park, walk inside the golf shop. If you choose to take your golf bag, do not take it in the golf shop. There will be a place outside to "park" your clubs. You will find clothing and golf equipment for sale in the golf shop. An employee (sometimes a golf instructor) will be behind the counter. Just let him or her know that you will be using the practice green.

If they are not busy, take the time to ask questions about

the golf course, fees, and whether they have ladies leagues or groups to play with, and if they have a dress code. If you are only going to the practice area to putt, you would not need to purchase a bucket of practice golf balls, just bring your own—we will explain putting in a minute. Most of the time the putting practice green area will be obvious, but if you are unsure, ask an employee.

There are also some standalone driving ranges where there is no golf course. Standalone driving ranges might or might not have an area to practice putting. You will start with putting, so if the driving range does not have an area to practice putting, find another venue.

Your learning adventure is organized by levels. Many golf instruction programs expect that because you are an adult, that you have certain physical skills. Our approach is more like martial arts. Just because you are an adult, the martial arts instructor does not expect you to break the board at your first class. We do not expect you to smash the ball hundreds of yards down the fairway on your first outing. You can progress through the levels as quickly as your schedule and your body will permit. Golf requires discipline and effort to be successful. Sounds a lot like life, doesn't it?

Level #1: Putting

Start with the end in mind.

—Stephen Covey

Seven Habits of Highly Effective People

The Hole is the Goal

Golf has many life lessons. If you know where you are going, it is easier to get there. The best way to learn golf is starting at the finish line (the hole in the ground), and working back to the starting line (the tee box where you will start each hole).

Equipment Needed: putter, golf ball, tennis ball, alignment sticks (ruler or yard sticks)

We start with putting. Putting is done on the closely mowed ground (the green), where there is a hole. The hole will have a flagstick in it. The hole is the "finish line" or the goal of each hole. The golf club we use is the PUTTER.

Putters come in many shapes and sizes (see photo).

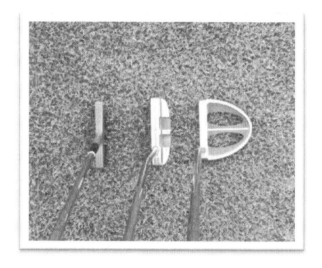

Blade, Blade, Mallot

The practice green has several holes for practice. A green on the golf course has only one hole. Of course, you probably already noticed this in your first assignment—watch golf on TV.

Alignment

Put the alignment sticks on the ground (see photo) and create a highway to the hole.

Stand parallel facing the sticks. This is how your body needs to stand when you are using the putter or any other club. Can you visualize a "highway" to the hole?

Putting Grip

Notice that the putter grip will have a flat side. Hold the grip with your thumbs on the flat surface pointing down the grip toward the ground (see photo). Most golfers putt with the right hand low. Some putt with their left hand low. Experiment to see which feels more comfortable.

Hands with thumbs down, right

hand lower on the handle

Hands with thumbs down, left hand
lower on the handle

Stand with your feet about shoulder-width apart or less and put the golf ball in the middle of your stance. Place the golf ball between the alignment sticks. Place your hands on the putter grip with your thumbs pointing down the grip toward the ground.

The Putting Stroke

Remember what it felt like when you stood in front of that full-length mirror and imitated the professionals' putting stroke? It's time for you to try it with a putter and a golf ball.

Swing your arms gently back and forth, strike the golf ball, and send it down the line into the hole. If you can count to two, you can putt. The backswing motion is one (1) and the forward motion is two (2). Let the acceleration come naturally as you go back and forth. Be sure to not let your legs move; they stay planted firmly on the ground as you "swing" the putter. Continue "putting" from various locations and distances around the hole. Putting is a big part of the golf game, so it is extremely important to practice.

Back Swing

Forward Swing

112

If you just can't get the hang of putting, do this remedial training. Take about six giant steps away from one of the holes on the putting green. Turn and face the hole. Starting with the tennis ball, roll it with your hand and try to have it stop right at the hole. Do that several times until you are able to get it within a 1-foot circle around the hole. Now roll the golf ball to the hole with your hand until you can get it to within a 1-foot circle around the hole. As you are doing this, notice if the ball was rolling uphill, downhill, or sloping to one side or the other. Notice how it affects the ball. Now try it after taking only three giant steps from the hole. How big is your arm swing with six giant steps versus three giant steps?

Putting Skills Test

Sink three of three putts from 3 feet away. Sink two of three putts from 5 feet away. Sink one of three putts from 10 feet away.

When you can pass this skills test, move to Level 2.

Always make putting part of your practice and warmup.

Preliminary Background before Starting Level 2

Before you take bigger swings with other golf clubs, there is important basic information that you need to know. This applies to the rest of the clubs that you will use.

Let's take a good look at the golf club and learn some lingo. The **golf club** has three basic parts. The **grip** is the end of the club that has either leather or a synthetic material wrapped around it. The **shaft** is the middle part that is either made of steel or graphite material. The **head** is the part that actually makes contact with the golf ball.

The head of the club also has three parts. The **heel** is where the shaft is attached, the **toe** is at the far end, and the **face** is in the middle where you will notice grooves. The face of each club will have a different amount of loft. Loft is your friend! Loft makes the ball go up in the air.

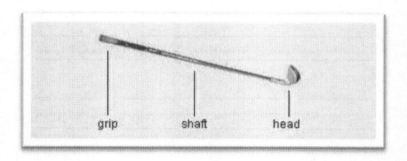

Parts of a golf club

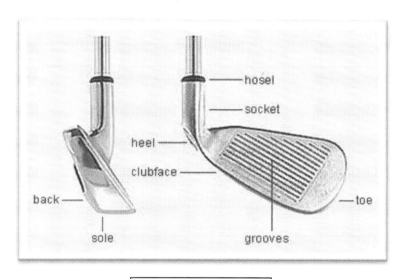

Parts of a golf club head

Holding (Gripping) the Club

You can use a yardstick as a guide. Thumbs and fingers wrap around the golf club in a similar matter. There are three classic golf grips: 10 finger, where all fingers and thumbs are on the club, or interlocking, where the little finger and index finger interlock or overlap

116

(two different ways to interlock the fingers are shown

in the bottom two photos)

Holding club with all 10 fingers wrapped around the handle

Holding club with 2 fingers interlocked on handle

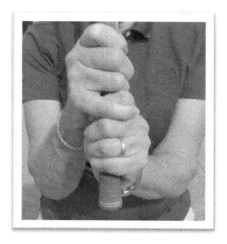

Holding handle with 2 fingers overlapping on handle

118

On the forward side of your hands, notice the lines between your thumbs and pointer fingers of each hand. We want both "lines" to point to our right shoulder. That will help our hands work together when swinging the golf club. The lines will be the same whatever grip you choose to use.

"V's" pointing to your right shoulder

Posture

To get in position to hit the ball, hinge (or bend) forward at the hips. The amount of hinge is determined by the length of the golf club. Long clubs, such as the driver, require less bend. Shorter clubs, such as the irons, require more bend. Back stays relatively straight. Knees are slightly bent. Arms hang down under the shoulders. Don't allow your shoulders to round too far forward. Keep your head in line with the spine; don't allow your head to hang down.

Golf Posture

The golf ball should be placed 1–2 feet in front of you, in the middle of your stance. This varies depending on the length of the club. Now practice!

Level #2: Chipping & Putting

(30–45 Minutes or Pass Skills Challenge)

Equipment Needed

putter, 7 iron, tennis balls, six golf balls, alignment sticks

(ruler or yard stick) , two small hand towels

Practice Area – Be Aware!

Some practice facilities have several areas to practice the short game. There might be a green used **only** for putting. There might be a separate green for chipping and pitching. If it's not obvious, just ask someone who works at the course.

Your next question should be, "How do I get the ball

onto the GREEN?"

Your first thought might be—*Can I use the PUTTER?* If you notice, the grass around the green isn't mowed quite as nicely as the green. That doesn't mean you can't putt, just think of it as putting over shag carpeting onto linoleum.

If the longer grass is going to interfere with a rolling golf ball, putting might not be a good option. You need to learn how to swing another club to get the ball over the longer grass and onto the green.

This is called **chipping**.

A warmup is recommended to get your body and brain processing speed and distance. Take the two towels and place them about two giant steps onto the green about 3 feet apart. Next take about three giant steps away from the green. From there, toss the tennis balls with your hand (one at a time!) and try to toss them so they land between the two towels.

After a few tosses, change to golf balls and try to toss them to the same spot on the green, between the two towels. Using the towels trains you to aim at a landing area. The hole is the ultimate goal, however, with chipping, it's important to establish a landing zone. Pay attention to how far the ball rolls after it hits the landing zone.

Set up your highway to the target by placing the alignment stick on the ground pointing to the spot between the two towels. Stand facing the alignment stick so you are setup parallel to it. This is how you will stand when swinging the 7 iron. See the photos for reference.

Chipping Set Up with an aiming stick and 2

towels as a target zone for landing the ball

Tom Watson

Now you are ready to use the 7 iron.

Get into a good posture. Shift your weight slightly

toward the target. This will help keep the lower body still

127

and make sure that the club is descending as it impacts the ball. Believe it or not, hitting down on the ball makes it go up!!

Set Up for Chipping looking face on

Let's talk about your breasts—if you have large ones. As you start to make bigger swings, they might get in the way. I have heard some "guys" say "Take them along for the ride." Obviously they don't have big breasts, and don't realize that this is not too comfortable. Here is a recommended solution for right-handed golfers: right arm under/left arm over. That allows the arms to raise the golf club in the back swing and down again for impact and follow through.

Swing the 7 iron back and forth in a pendulum fashion, just like the one-two tempo of the putting stroke. It requires a little more energy, because we are sending the golf ball a little farther. Your goal is to swing and send the golf ball so it lands between the two towels we have placed on the green. On your practice swing, you should see that you are brushing the grass in the middle where the golf ball will be sitting. After you can successfully brush the grass, place a golf ball there and swing. The ball should gently "toss" onto the green, close to the towels. Your arms will remain straight (but not stiff) through the swing.

Chipping Back Swing

Chipping Forward Swing

130

Next, chip toward a hole. Pick a hole that is about 20 feet away from the edge of the green. Take one step off the green, and practice chipping from there. Your goal is to have the ball go up in the air over the long grass, land on the green, and roll to within a giant step of the hole. Once you have done this successfully 50 percent of the time, take two steps off the green. Practice from different spots.

Be brave and step back another three giant steps from the green and go through the same process again. Practice this until you can land half of your shots in the target range. For some of you this might only take a short time—for others, it might take several sessions.

Keys to remember:

• Keep your weight on your target side, with your body staying steady.

• Arms stay long.

• Wrists stay firm.

131

Troubleshooting the Chip (Skip this section if your chips are good.)

Problem: No loft on ball.

Solution—Keep your swing inside the "highway." Brush the grass where the ball is sitting. Club should be descending as the ball is contacted.

Problem: Ball going right or left.

Solution—The ball travels in the direction that the face of the club strikes the ball, so make sure the bottom edge of the club is lined up down the dotted line of the highway.

Here are pictures of what your golf club will look like and where the ball will go.

Club Face "Open" – Ball Goes Right

Club Face "Square" – Ball Goes Straight

Club Face "Closed" – Ball Goes Left

*This concept will apply to all golf clubs you will use while golfing.

Chipping and Putting Together

Go back to the chipping practice exercise. This time after you have chipped on the green, finish by putting the ball in the hole. Start to keep track of the number of strokes it takes to get the ball in the hole. Two is great, three is good, four average—more than four means you need more practice. Any time you are struggling, go back to the basic drills of tossing the ball. Even professional golfers use some simple drills to get them back on track. I have attended many professional golf tournaments and have observed most of the professionals using alignment sticks when they are warming up. So don't be self-conscious about using tools to help you do things correctly and improve more quickly.

Skills Challenge

Choose a hole that is about 20 feet from the edge of the green. Take a giant step off of the green. Chip the ball onto the green, and then putt it into the designated hole. Keep track of your strokes. Get the ball in the hole in four strokes or less. Do this three times in a row. You are now ready for Level 3.

Level #3: Pitching, Chipping, & Putting

(30–45 Minutes or Pass Skills Challenge)

Equipment Needed

putter, 7 iron, pitching wedge (PW or P on the bottom of the club), tennis balls, racquet, alignment sticks

Start the session with 5 minutes of putting practice. Start close to the hole and move farther away as you make the putts. Then, practice chipping for 5 minutes with a 7 iron. Use the towels for "targets" on the green. Next use the pitching wedge. You'll need to stand a little closer to the ball, because this club is a little shorter than the 7 iron. You should notice that the ball goes higher and does not roll as far.

Chipping and pitching are often confusing. For chipping—imagine to keep it low and let it roll—using a 7 iron. For pitching—imagine flying it high and letting it stop—using a pitching wedge.

Gradually—giant step by giant step—move farther from the target until you get about 30 giant steps away. Use both the 7 iron and pitching wedge. You will reach a point (approximately six to seven paces) where it is difficult to keep the 7 iron on the green. At that point just use the pitching wedge. Keep your weight evenly distributed. Make slightly bigger swings as you move farther from the green. Allow your wrists to hinge in the backswing. On the downswing, the wrists unhinge, and you follow through, a little above waist height. Hold the finish. You are now "pitching" the ball. The ball flies higher and lands softer than a chip.

Pitching Set Up

Pitching Back Swing --------------------- Pitching Forward Swing

If you are having difficulty, practice tossing tennis balls onto the green. After tossing the tennis balls, use the tennis racket. Swing the racket in an underhand fashion.

Try tossing golf balls onto the green using the racket. You can move a little closer or a little farther from the green to get a feeling of how much swing you really have to do to get the ball on the green (and stay on the green)! Once you have had success with the racket, pick up your pitching wedge again and give it a try.

Pitching Practice

Take five giant steps from the green. Your goal is to have the ball go up in the air over the long grass, land on the green, and stay on the green. Once you have done this successfully 50 percent of the time, take 10 giant steps from the green and repeat. Practice from different spots.

The next step combines pitching, chipping, and putting. Choose a hole on the practice surface as your target. Take 20 giant steps away from the green. Use the pitching wedge to pitch the ball as close to the hole as possible. If your ball remains on the green, use your putter to finish. If your ball is short of the green or rolls off, you can choose to pitch the ball again, or chip with your 7 iron to get it on the green. Keep score. Two— awesome, three—great, four—good, five—average, and six—need more practice.

Skills Challenge

Pick a hole on the green. Take 20 giant steps away from the green. Use pitching, chipping, and putting to get the ball in the hole in five or fewer strokes. Do this two times in a row. You are ready for Level 4.

If you need more practice, don't be discouraged. Pitching and chipping are difficult. If you watch professional golf on television, you will quickly notice that even the professionals make mistakes around the green.

Congratulations! You are developing a repertoire of golf shots.

Level #4: Full-Swing Preparation

Smashing Balls—Oh Yeah!

Equipment Needed

7 iron, tee-ball stand, plastic bat, whiffle ball or foam balls, medium-size bouncing ball

Let's be clear—you do not have to be physically fit to play golf. You can ride in a golf cart, drink beer, smoke cigarettes, never break a sweat, and still be a really good golfer. However, if you want to minimize the risk of injury and extend your playing career, we have a few recommendations. After all, we want this journey to last a lifetime, a long lifetime.

Up to this point, the short game has tested your

coordination and skill, but it has not tested the speed and strength of your muscles.

Before we get to the full swing, it's a great idea to get the muscles moving and practice some movement patterns to make your learning experience more efficient and successful.

Warm Up the Muscles

A warmup should be done at the golf course or at home before starting your golf game or a practice or learning session. If you feel any **PAIN** at any time, **STOP!** Ten years ago, it was unusual to see golfers stretching, exercising, or warming up. Things have changed—and fitness is considered an integral part of the game.

Standing Arm Rotation

Standing with your feet shoulder width apart, extend your arms out in front of you. Keeping your balance and feet stable, rotate your right arm to the back of you, until it is in line with your left arm. Hold for 3 seconds. Repeat with the left arm rotating to your back until it is in line with your right arm.

A-Frame Open

Bend from your hip sockets, putting your elbow on one knee and your hand on the other. Reach behind you, pointing your arm vertically in the air. Feel the stretch in your shoulder and upper back. Repeat on the opposing side.

Helicopter Lunges

Holding your arms out by your side with elbows locked, step into a good lunge (front knee over the front ankle and trunk upright). From here, rotate your upper body back and forth for 15 seconds, but keep your head facing forward. Make sure your weight stays centered over your front foot; don't let your weight shift to the outside of your foot. Repeat on the other side.

Arm Circles

Thumbs up—hold arms out to the side——circle arms forward in small, then medium, then large circles. Then circle arms backward—large, medium, and small. Repeat with thumbs pointing forward, then thumbs down.

Leg Swings

Swing leg forward and backward. Then swing leg out to the side like you are getting on a horse, and then swing it back like you are getting off the horse. Repeat on the other side. Try to keep upper body centered.

Leg Swings

Windmill

Stand with your arms out parallel to the ground and feet shoulder width apart. Bow forward about 45 degrees. Slowly turn to the right and let your left hand point at the ground about 2 feet in front of you. Repeat on the other side. Repeat this motion three times.

This warm-up routine should take about 5 minutes.

Movement for Golf

Most instructional books and golf professionals skip over this next step. You can skip it, but it has been our experience that it expedites the learning process exponentially. You don't need to go to the golf course to do this. You can do it in your backyard, living room, or at a gym or the park.

You might feel a little self-conscious doing these activities. I have just three words for you—GET OVER IT!! Relax, learn to PLAY again.

"We don't stop playing because we grow old;

we grow old because we stop playing."

—George Bernard Shaw

I have taught hundreds of women to play golf during the

past 10 years. Two years ago we developed the Smashing Balls methodology, and the time to learn golf decreased dramatically. Most important, the ladies who used this methodology have stuck with golf.

If you are not athletic, the following movements will get you prepared for golf. Initially it might take a lot of effort physically, and also mentally. As you become more proficient, the movements occur without so much thinking. This is important, because the golf swing occurs in seconds. The movements need to be automatic. Thinking occurs before you step up to hit the ball. Once you are in position to hit the ball, your mind can hold from zero to one thought to have a successful golf swing. If you can clear your mind to zero thoughts—congratulations! You were probably a Zen master in a previous life. Most of us have to focus on one thought or phrase. Yours is likely to be unique to you. Some classic thoughts are counting "1, 2." Some use the word "focus."

If you grew up and played any sports, such as tennis, softball, or field hockey, you will have ***movement skills that are important in the golf swing***. Even if you have participated in these sports, it's still a good idea to reawaken these movement patterns. Make no mistake, creating a good golf swing is difficult, and you will want to do everything you can to make it easier.

In addition to describing the exercise, I have explained the reason that it is important. If you don't care why you are doing the exercise, feel free to skip over this part. I have included it for the engineers, accountants, and those who need to know why.

This process will take about 10 to 15 minutes!

Tee Ball Striking

Not much to explain here. Smash these balls as hard and far as you can. We found some sponge balls at the store and an inexpensive tee-ball stand and plastic bat.

Why—Let's face it, if you can't hit a big ball with a big bat, you don't stand a chance to hit a little ball with a little club. Start with bigger balls and work your way down to smaller balls. You will know you are ready for a smaller ball when you can hit four out of five well.

A big problem for women learning to golf is that they swing slowly to make sure that they make contact with the little ball. Tee-ball striking gets some swing speed and eye-hand coordination going. Besides, it's a blast!

If you have had a bad day, picture your least favorite person's face on the ball, and smash it. This is a great stress reliever!

Do this activity for 5 minutes.

Back-to-Back Ball Pass

Using a lightweight ball, stand back to back with your partner. The first person holds the ball out in front of them with both hands and turns to the right and passes the ball to your partner, extending your arms, she takes the ball and continues the circle and passes the ball back to you (on the

left side)

If you are by yourself, stand with your back to the wall. Extend your arms. Twist to the right and have the ball touch the wall. Let the ball turn in your hands so that the right hand is on the bottom and the left hand is on top.

Then twist to the left and touch the wall. Let the ball turn in your hands so that the left hand is on the bottom and the right hand is on top. Keep your lower body as still as you can.

Why—This movement gets a rotary motion going. This creates a more powerful and athletic swing. Too many women try to hit the golf ball by swaying straight back and sliding forward, Sliding and swaying produces a weak swing and makes your knees, back, shoulders, and elbows more susceptible to injury.

This exercise helps develop stability in the lower body and flexibility in the upper body. It also gets the hands rolling over in the proper fashion.

Do this for 1 to 2 minutes. Bonus—it's great for the waistline!

Ball Bounce

Using the lightweight ball, stand about 5 feet from your partner. Turn sideways and bounce the ball to your partner. If 5 feet is too easy, move farther away.

Use some force to bounce the ball. Try to bounce the ball over their head.

Do this facing right and facing left.

If you are by yourself, bounce the ball against a wall.

Why—To develop speed and rotary power in the core muscles, and it's kind of fun!

Do this for 1 to 2 minutes.

Balance Practice

Using a golf club or the back of a chair or your partner's shoulders for support (no injuries please!) balance on one leg. Hold for 30 seconds, up to 1 minute. Be brave and try it with your eyes closed.

Why—When you make a golf swing, your weight should shift from your back leg to your front leg. If you have poor balance, transferring the weight can be difficult. Balance is a great life skill. Falls are a major problem with the elderly. Practicing balance can prevent falls!

Practice 1 to 2 minutes.

Overhead Deep Squat

Stand with your arms holding a golf club high overhead. Slowly lower yourself to a chair or bench, just touching and then slowly rise up. If it is too difficult, fold your arms across your chest and try the deep squat. Remember slowly down and slowly up.

Why—This exercise develops lower body power and upper body flexibility, which are critical to a good golf swing.

So we spent 5 minutes warming up your body and 10 minutes on warm-up movement skills.

Once you are successfully smashing the golf ball, the functional movement exercises have done their job, and you don't really need to continue to do them. However, you should participate in exercise programs that stress flexibility, balance, and strength for the core and lower body.

Level #4: (Continued)
Smashing the Ball with a Full   Swing

Equipment Needed

tees, 7 iron, alignment sticks , range balls (purchased at
the pro shop)

Optional—Hula Hoop, golf glove (a glove can make it
easier to grip the club, especially if you play in hot, humid
conditions. One glove is usually worn on the non-dominant
hand—that is, if you play golf right handed, the glove goes
on the left hand).

It seems like we've gone through quite a lot to get this point. Just like many life and work situations, preparation makes the performance much better.

You are ready for the driving range . . . not the NASCAR racetrack, but the range where you get to smash golf balls as hard as you can!

Every golf club you swing on the range should be swung with robust, smashing energy. Your gentle chipping, pitching, and putting were all on or near the green. Now we are trying to advance the golf ball as far as we can. For now, we are going to stick with the 7 iron until you can hit the ball 75 yards.

Swing Shape

If you need a visual, the Hula Hoop is the shape of your golf swing. Set the Hula Hoop up on edge. Tilt it back and forth and see how just one point touches the ground. Stand in your golf posture with your arms hanging from your shoulders and rest the Hula Hoop on your arms. The Hula Hoop rests on the ground at the position of the golf ball.

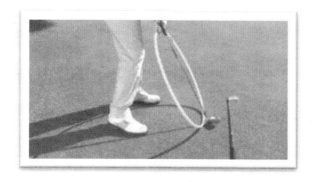

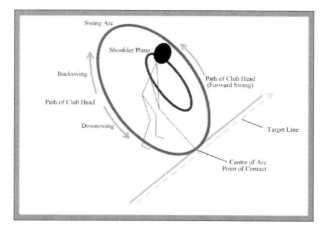

I hope this picture doesn't make you dizzy! It is just meant to show you the circle or arc that the club AND your body create when swinging the golf club.

This will give you an idea of the shape of your golf swing and the path the golf club should travel.

We need to create that highway to the finish line that we have been utilizing in putting, chipping, and pitching, using a few of your golf clubs. Use alignment sticks to create the highway to the target—maybe flags or signs located in the driving range.

Full Swing Set up

Start practicing your position to address the ball and to grip the golf club. Place a golf tee in the middle of the highway. Push the tee about halfway into the ground, so that half the tee is in the air. Use this as your practice position. After you are comfortable getting into the address position, let's take some small swings (like the chip or pitch) and knock the tee out of the ground. Start with a small swing and with each successful swing (knocking the tee out of the ground) increase the size of the back and forth. As the swing gets bigger, your arms bring the club up and down and your body turns right and left. The turn is going to feel like a combination of the windmill warm-up exercise and tee-ball smashing.

Small Back Swing

Medium Back Swing

Full Back Swing

If you are confused, stop and do the windmill exercise again right there. The only difference is that we have our arms hanging down from our shoulders holding the golf club. They will form a "Y" with the tee or golf ball at the point on the ground where the club rests. As we make the body turn to the right (for right handed golfers) AND keep your perfect golf posture your arms raise up bringing the club up also to a position near your shoulder or ear......remember to keep that left arm as straight as possible.

Small Swing

Medium Swing

174

Full Swing

We are still knocking the tee out of the ground with each smashing swing. Remember to finish your swing and hold the pose just like the professional golfers.

Finish positions

Catrina Mathews

Nancy Lopez
176

Mickey Wright

We need to see it, feel what that position is all about, and then do it, repeatedly. Every swing you make should end by holding a balanced position with your belly button aimed at the target for a 5-second count—out loud! **If you didn't finish like this, move into that position, and hold for the 5-second count**. This is your own biofeedback training.

Once that tee comes out of the ground 8 out of 10 swings,

you are ready to use a golf ball! If you are good at knocking the tee out of the ground, you're likely to be successful hitting the golf ball off the ground. Some driving ranges are not as manicured as others and there might not be much grass. If this is the case, put the golf ball on a tee that is pushed into the ground so just the top of the tee is showing. Your goal is to hit the ball with the 7 iron for a minimum of 75 yards. Once you've done that, it's show time—let's play golf!

Level #5: Play Modified Golf

Equipment Needed

tees, a golf bag (keep it light), golf balls (six or more), Sharpie marking pen, 7 iron, pitching wedge, putter, ball marker (a coin will work).

Optional—golf glove

You might put off playing golf until you think you're good enough—**big mistake**. Just as in the business world, women wait until they think they are 100 percent qualified for a promotion to apply, while men go after promotions when they meet 60 percent of the qualifications. Don't wait. If you have met the skill challenges outlined in the previous levels, you are ready to go.

This session's primary goal is to familiarize you with the golf course, etiquette, and a few rules. Secondary, there will be some ball smashing, pitching, chipping, and putting. There is a lot to learn without concerning yourself with which club to select, so you're only going to use a 7 iron, pitching wedge, and putter for now.

Before you get to the course, familiarize yourself with the following section on etiquette and abbreviated rules.

You might think of golf as smashing the ball, and watching it travel great distances, but golf is much more than that. Etiquette and a code of conduct are as important as the actual ball-striking part of the game.

The official rule book for golf starts with etiquette. Golf is considered a gentlemen and ladies game. What's the difference between etiquette and the rules of golf? An example—talking while another player is playing is not against the rules, but it is considered poor etiquette. If you are playing with more experienced players, ask them to tell you if you are not following proper etiquette.

The United States Golf Association (USGA) has issued the following guidance that you should be familiar with before you play for the first time. The major categories are spirit of the game, consideration of other players, and care of the course.

The Spirit of the Game

Golf is played, for the most part, without the supervision of a referee or umpire. The game relies on the integrity of the individual to show consideration for other players and to abide by the rules. All players should conduct themselves in a disciplined manner, demonstrating courtesy and sportsmanship at all times, irrespective of how competitive they might be. This is the spirit of the game of golf.

Safety

Players should ensure that no one is standing close by or

in a position to be hit by the club, the ball, or any stones, pebbles, twigs, or the like when they make a stroke or practice swing.

Players should not play until the players in front are out of range.

If your ball is going in a direction where there is a danger of hitting someone, immediately shout FORE at the top of your lungs.

Consideration for Other Players

Players should always show consideration for other players on the course and should not disturb their play by moving, talking, or making unnecessary noise.

Players should ensure that any electronic device, such as a cell phone, does not distract other players.

Players should not stand close to or directly behind the ball, or directly behind the hole, when a player is about to play.

On the Putting Green

On the putting green, players should not stand on another player's line of putt or, when she is making a stroke, cast a shadow over her line of putt.

Etiquette: Shadow on Putting Line

https://www.youtube.com/watch?v=yjd_k_jno9U

Players should remain on or close to the putting green until all other players in the group have holed out.

Pace of Play

Players should play at a good pace. Play when safe play when ready.

It is a group's responsibility to keep up with the group in front. If one group is delaying the group behind, it should invite the group behind to play through (in other words, pass your group), irrespective of the number of players in that group.

Be Ready to Play

Players should be ready to play as soon as it is their turn to play. The player farthest from the hole is first to play. When playing on or near the putting green, they should leave their bags or carts in such a position as will enable quick movement off the green and toward the next tee. When the play of a hole has been completed, players should immediately leave the putting green.

Lost Ball

If a player believes his ball might be lost outside a water hazard or is out of bounds, to save time, he should play a second ball—this is called a provisional ball.

Players searching for a ball should signal the players in the group behind them to play through as soon as it becomes apparent that the ball will not easily be found. Five minutes is the time limit for searching for a ball.

Care of the Course

Bunkers (Sand Trap)

Before leaving a bunker, players should carefully fill up and smooth over all holes and footprints made by them and any nearby made by others, with a rake if available.

https://www.youtube.com/watch?v=8hIRLVqYGW4

Repair of Divots, Ball Marks

Players should carefully repair any divot (clump of grass) holes made by them. Fill divot holes with the divot, or sand. Repair damage to the putting green made by the impact of a ball as demonstrated in the following picture. You can use a ball mark repair tool, or a tee to repair the damage. Pull

187

the grass back over the damaged area and tap level with the

bottom of your putter.

Repairing Green Divot

https://www.youtube.com/watch?v=56G_cmZiyjM

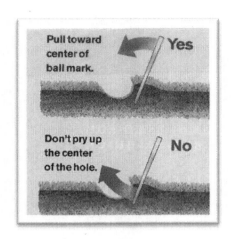

Pull toward center of ball mark.

Yes

Don't pry up the center of the hole.

No

Preventing Unnecessary Damage

Players should ensure that no damage is done to the putting green when putting down bags or the flagstick. Bags are placed on the side of the green.

In order to avoid damaging the hole, players and caddies should not stand too close to the hole.

Golf Carts

Local notices regulating the movement of golf carts should be strictly observed. Stay at least 30 yards from the greens. The 90-degree rule refers to driving the golf cart on the designated cart path for each hole. When you get adjacent to your golf ball, you drive out onto the fairway, hit your shot, and then drive back to the path and continue to the green using the cart path.

The golf cart should remain on the cart path on most par 3s.

I hope we didn't put you to sleep with all those rules/disclaimers/etiquette. Once you start your journey playing golf, you will see how important these are. "Royal and Ancient" was the original rules governing body, and still has precedence in European Golf, and along with the USGA, they take great care in preserving this great game of golf. There are many more rules for situations on the golf course, but this is enough to get you started.

Some other rules you will encounter are out of bounds, red hazard, yellow hazard, proper drop of a golf ball, unplayable lie, obstructions, immoveable obstructions, etc.

You'll learn much of this with experience. Don't worry about it for now.

Level 5 Action Items

Decide where to play. If you have access to a par-3 course, or executive course (they are shorter), start there. By now, you've established a rapport with the employees where you have been practicing. Ask them for a recommendation.

A few days before you want to play, make a tee time. This involves calling a golf course or going online and booking the time. You can even do it in person at the golf shop. Most courses do not schedule more than seven days out.

Be prepared to answer the following questions:

What day of the week do you want to play? What time of day?

As a newer golfer, ask the golf shop for a time when there are not many golfers on the course. Normally later in the day is less crowded. This will make your first experience more pleasant. It should be less expensive to play later in the day. This is a basic supply-and-demand economics lesson. There is more demand for morning tee times, so it is more expensive.

How many players will there be?

You can go by yourself or with friends. The golf course typically allows four golfers for each starting time. If you have fewer than four players, a complete stranger might join your group. I always hope for George Clooney, but that hasn't happened yet. Playing with strangers can be intimidating, but that's part of the golf adventure!

Will you be walking or riding?

Some golf courses do not give you the option. Using a golf cart will have more dos and don'ts, so you might want to keep things simple and walk, if you have the option. You will also have to see how well you fill up your golf bag. If it is too heavy, you will want a golf cart. If you "pack light," walking can be fun, plus it's great exercise. Some golf courses have pull carts to rent. Eventually as you carry more clubs, you might want to have your own pull cart.

Will be you playing 9 or 18 holes?

Start with nine holes.

Your First Day on the Course!

Arrive at the golf course 30 to 45 minutes before your tee time.

Go to the pro shop and check in. Pick up a score card and pencil.

Normally there are restrooms on the course. The starter, or the person who checks you in, can give you the location.

Take 10 minutes to practice putting and chipping.

Do your warm up.

Go to the first tee with your group about 7 to 10 minutes before your tee time.

(Sometimes there will be a starter at the first tee. He makes sure everyone is going in the proper order. Later in the day, a starter might not be present.)

If you don't already know your playing partners, introduce yourself. Let them know that you are a beginner, and that you will be making some modifications to maintain a good pace of play.

Good golfers can enjoy playing with beginner golfers. Nobody likes playing with a slow golfer, so keep it moving.

Use the Sharpie pen to make a distinguished mark on your ball. The mark can be dots, a line, or an initial. Pay attention to the type of ball (Titleist or Callaway) and the number on the ball. It's really embarrassing if you hit someone else's ball, so identify your ball before you play it. It also results in a penalty.

At the first tee box, there will be multiple sets of tees. Right now we are going to strongly suggest a modification.

You are going to go directly to the 150-yard marker. It's usually marked with a white pole or a white marker. Eventually you will hit from the most forward tees, but not on your first outing.

Tee Box Explanation

https://www.youtube.com/watch?v=SsznmAFy2cI

Use your 7 iron to hit the ball off the ground, if you have

been successful doing that at the driving range. If not, tee the ball up. If you have been hitting the ball with your 7 iron for 75 yards or more, you should be able to get to the green in two or three shots. When you get close enough to the green, use your chipping and pitching shots. MODIFICATION—If you are not on the green by your fourth shot, pick it up, and drop it on the edge of the green.

Use your putter to putt the ball into the hole. MODIFICATION—After four putts, pick the ball up and move to the next hole. ETIQUETTE—When you are on the green and waiting for others to putt, it is appropriate to "mark" your ball. Marking the ball consists of placing a small object like a coin behind the ball. After the ball is marked, you pick it up. You can clean it if it is dirty. When it is your turn to putt, place the ball in front of the marker, and pick up the marker.

Marking My Golf Ball

https://www.youtube.com/watch?v=oIxvfUQAEOM

Replacing Marker

https://www.youtube.com/watch?v=Z25njqBKl-I

Reminder—do not cast a shadow or walk in other players' lines. The first player to hole out, normally replaces the flag after everyone has made their putts.

A few other MODIFICATIONS—if you are in the sand, pull the ball out and drop it next to the sand bunker. Count lifting the ball from the sand as a stroke and keep moving. We'll cover sand shots in later.

Keep score by counting those strokes you take from the tee box to the hole. For more on scoring and the scorecard see the Appendix. In a MODIFIED game, the most strokes recommended for one hole is eight. We are doing this to keep up the pace of play.

There's a lot to observe on the golf course as you play this MODIFIED game.

- The grass will be mowed shorter in a path between the teeing area and the green. This is the **fairway**.

- On the sides of the fairway, the grass will be longer. This is the **rough**.

- You might notice **markings** in the fairway and sometimes on the car path. Normally a blue marker is 200 yards from the green, white is 150, and red is 100. The sprinkler heads might also give you the yardage to the green.

- The **flags** might be different colors. Red is at the front of the green, white in the middle, and blue on the back of the green. This is not always the case, but it is fairly standard.

After you've completed nine holes, shake hands with your playing partners. Congratulate yourself on getting out there. Experience is a great teacher, and you've learned a tremendous amount.

You are ready for Level 6 when you can score 55 or less in the MODIFIED format. **If you don't have time to play nine holes, go back to the other levels for more practice. Various practice games are listed in the Appendix to keep your practice interesting and fun.**

Level #6: Adding Clubs

Equipment Needed: driver, 4 or 5 hybrid club, 7 iron, 9

iron, pitching wedge

As with any practice session, start with 10 minutes of putting and chipping.

Then off to the driving range for the next 20 to 30 minutes.

Start with your familiar 7 iron. At this point in your young golf career, the 7 iron should be allowing your ball to travel somewhere between 75 to 100 yards.

Skills Challenge—Before you introduce other clubs, you should be hitting the ball 75–100 yards with your 7 iron, three of five times before you introduce other clubs.

If you don't have consistency with the 7 iron, introducing more clubs has the potential to make golf even more complicated.

Once you know how far your 7 iron travels consistently, we can introduce other clubs. Each club increment should be about a 10-yard difference. So for example, if you hit your 7 iron 100 yards, your 8 iron should go 90 yards, and your 9 iron 80 yards. You get the idea. Establish a baseline with your 7 iron and figure out other club distances from there.

When you are comfortable hitting irons, next try the hybrid club, and then the driver. When you practice hitting the driver, tee it up. The top of the tee should be about an inch and a half to two inches above the ground.

Level #7: Special Shots

15 Minutes—Combine This Level with another Level

Where You Need Practice, Such as Putting and Chipping

Equipment Needed: sand wedge (S or SW on the bottom of

the club), balls, putter

Getting Out of the Sand

Believe it or not you've already done this shot. And as Chi Chi Rodriguez says, "It's the easiest shot in golf. You don't even need to hit the ball."

This shot is similar to the pitch shot. You just simply hit slightly behind the ball, and let the sand carry the ball out of the bunker. Begin with a drill that shows you where you strike the sand. Draw 2 parallel lines perpendicular to your "highway to the hole" in the sand. Take some swings catching the line closest to your right foot and see if you carve out sand as far as the line closest to your left foot. The photo shows snakes on those parallel lines. Practice this several times and then you can place a golf ball anywhere inside those 2 parallel lines and the sand will propel the ball out of the bunker. The key is to stay relaxed as you swing, let the club carry the sand and golf ball out of the bunker.

Important Rule—When you are in a bunker, you cannot touch the sand with your club before the swing. If you take a practice swing, do not touch the sand. It is advisable to take your practice swing before you enter the bunker.

Sand Drill with 2 lines

Overhead view of sand shot set up

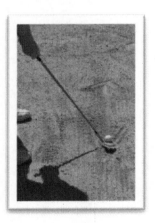

Sand view down the line

Level #8: Golf, the Real Thing

Equipment Needed: clubs, balls, tees, ball marker.

Optional—glove

You should be relieved that the instructions are getting less complicated and verbose. You've learned a ton of information about golf. Not only smashing the ball, but rules and etiquette—way to go!

Refer to Level 5—Set up a tee time. We still recommend playing late in the day or when the course is not crowded. Nine holes is enough the first few times out.

This time, take more clubs. I suggest a putter, sand wedge, pitching wedge, 9 iron, 7 iron, 5 hybrid, and driver.

This time play from the forward tee box. The preliminary levels have set the stage to make golf an enjoyable experience.

As in Level 5, keep score. However in an effort to up the pace of play, the same rules apply. If you are not on the green after four strokes, pick the ball up and put it on the green. Maximum putts should be four. Total score for a hole should not exceed eight. Until you score 55 or less, maintain this scoring system. When playing with others, simply tell them that you are using this scoring to maintain the pace of play.

You're ready for the next level when you can score less than 55 for nine holes.

Level #9: Opportunities for More Golf

SEARCH FOR BEGINNER leagues, and get into regular playing routine.

Depending on your comfort level, you might want to sign up to play in fundraising and company tournaments. Most of these types of tournaments are a scramble format. In this format, everyone tees off, the best shot is chosen, and everyone plays from there. You rarely wind up with a bad shot, and you can be a real hero if you are a good putter.

We can play golf for many years into our twilight time. Quality routines and practice create quality golf.

Keep Your Cup Empty

A young man had read all the books he could about Zen. He heard about a Zen master and requested an appointment with him to ask for teachings. When they were seated, the young man proceeded to tell the master everything he had understood from his reading, saying that Zen is about this and Zen is about that, on and on.

After some time, the master suggested that they have tea. He performed the traditional tea ceremony while the student sat at attention, bowing when served, and saying nothing. The master began to pour tea into the student's cup. He poured until it was full, and kept pouring. The tea ran over the edge of the cup and onto the table. The master kept pouring as tea ran off the table and onto the floor. Finally, the student couldn't contain himself any longer. He shouted,

"Stop! Stop pouring! The cup is full—no more will go in!"

The master stopped pouring and said, "Just like this cup, your mind is full of your own opinions and preconceptions. How can you learn anything unless you first empty your cup?"

—Dr. Joseph Parent, *Zen Golf*

When you started this adventure, your mind was empty regarding golf. As you continue to learn more about golf, keep an open mind about what is being communicated. Give new or different instructions a fair chance to see whether they work for you.

Play golf with honor and integrity, and doors will open for you.

Glossary

EQUIPMENT

Driver—The longest club and is commonly used on the tee box.

Fairway Woods—This club is used in the fairway. By the way, it is not made of wood, but metal material.

Hybrids—These are relatively new to golf. They are a cross between a fairway wood and an iron.

Irons—These are used in the fairway.

Putter—The putter design is either a blade or a mallet. It has the least loft of any club in your bag and is used on the green or wherever you feel you can roll the ball along the ground.

Wedges—The most lofted clubs in your set. These are used next to the green or in sand bunkers for those delicate shots.

Golf Club List

Drivers   Fairways   Hybrids   Irons   52° Wedge   56° Wedge   60° Wedge   Putters

COURSE BASICS

Bunker—Sand-filled area that is referred to as a hazard.

Divot—That large chunk of ground or turf that you or someone else displaced during your golf swing.

Dogleg—Refers to a fairway that bends.

Drive —The shot from the teeing ground.

Fairway—It is close-mowed turf running from tee to green.

Flag Stick and Cup—The hole in the ground where your goal is to get the ball inside.

Fringe—This is the grass all around the putting green. It is usually cut a little shorter than the fairway but not as short as the green.

217

Green—The shortest cut grass, where the cup and flag stick are located.

Rough—Area of long grass on either side of the fairway or around the green

Tee Box or the Teeing Ground—The starting place for the hole to be played. It is a rectangular area two club lengths in depth, the front and the sides of which are defined by the outside limits of two tee-markers.

GOLF SWING

Arc—The curved shape you are striving for in your golf swing.

Fat—This is hitting the ground before the golf ball ("big ball—earth; little ball—golf ball")

Full Swing—The shot using a full motion (full throttle) to hit (smash) the ball.

218

Whiff—This is a swing and a miss, hitting air instead of the golf ball.

The USGA publishes a rules book that is usually under $3.00. It can also be downloaded from www.usga.org. If you are going to continue to play, it's good to have on hand as a reference. Only a select few golfers really read and understand all of the nuances of the rules. Don't let that intimidate you. On the contrary, be aware that just because a golfer is a professional, or has been playing for a long time, doesn't make them an authority on the rules.

Appendix #1

THE SCORECARD & SCORING

Some scorecards will show a picture of each hole. The distance for each set of tees is listed. You will want to start from the most forward tee box—usually red. Score keeping is fairly simple. You count the number of strokes and record it. When you are first starting, you might not want to keep score. Remember pace of play is important for the enjoyment of everyone who shares the course with you.

You'll notice there is a men's handicap and a women's handicap assigned for each hole. This is an indicator of hole difficulty. The "1" handicap hole is considered the hardest hole on the front nine. On the scorecard pictured above, it is hole number 4.

We'll discuss handicap briefly. For most beginner golfers, a handicap is not something you should worry about. Once you start playing more often and have a good feel that you are playing under the USGA rules of golf, you can post scores that will calculate your handicap.

Your handicap is your potential as a golfer. It is the number of strokes a player might deduct from his actual score to "adjust" his score to the level of a scratch golfer. It is designed to allow golfers of different abilities to basically compete on the same level.

Example:

Alice has a handicap of 1

Zelda has a handicap of 11

- The stroke differential is 10. Zelda will get 10 strokes from Alice to adjust her score to Alice's level.

- Alice shoots a 77.

- Zelda shoots an 89 - 10 = 79.

- Zelda buys the drinks!

Par—This is the score that represents the number of strokes a skilled golfer would have on the golf hole. Each hole allows for some number of strokes based on the distance from the tee box to the green, and this would include two putting strokes to get the ball into the hole.

Birdie—This is playing the golf hole in one stroke under the par number.

Eagle—This is playing the golf hole in two strokes under the par number.

Hole in one is when you hit the golf ball from the tee

box and it goes in the hole! (You will now owe drinks to everyone in your group or the club house!)

Bogie is playing the golf hole in one stroke over the par number.

Double bogie is playing the golf hole in two strokes over the par number.

Triple/quadruple bogie, you get the picture.

The score card will also have course rating and slope numbers. Average course rating—72. Average slope—113. If the numbers are lower, the course is easier. For higher numbers, the course is more difficult.

Appendix #2

PRACTICE GAMES

PUTTING GAMES

Here are some putting games to make you a great putter and to keep you engaged in practice.

Circle Drill

Start 2 feet from the hole with six balls. Advance only after holing all six golf balls in a row. Move out 1 foot at a time.

Ladder Drill

This is to help you practice distance control. Set up six markers. These can be tees, ball markers, or any fun object. They should be positioned approximately 1 foot apart starting from the hole and forming the appearance of a ladder. The markers should be off to the left or right depending on your hand dominance. Putt from the first marker to the hole. If you make the putt, move on to the

second marker. If you make the next putt, move onto the next

marker, and so on. If you miss the putt or "fall off the ladder"

(with a soft landing, of course!) return to the first and attempt

to climb the ladder again. It's quite rewarding to reach the

top!

Ladder Drill

Penny Drill

Place a penny at the edge of the hole. Mark off 3 feet, 6 feet, and 9 feet putting distance from the cup. Use four golf balls. From 3 feet, putt three of four and roll over the penny to make the putt. From 6 feet, roll two out of four over the penny into the cup. And from 9 feet, roll one out of four into the cup. It must roll over the penny to count.

This drill causes you to focus with more precision.

Humpty Dumpty

Put five balls on golf tees in a row, about one golf ball width apart. Take a giant step back and with five golf balls, putt and try to knock the balls off the tees. You have five chances. After you get five out of five, move back another step and go for five out of five again. It might take a few tries, but you will soon fine tune your putting!

227

Humpty Dumpty

CHIPPING GAMES

Landing Zone/Distance Drill

Pick a spot about 6 to 8 feet off the green. Chip three balls to the same landing zone, having them come to rest within a 3-foot circle of one another. Repeat with three different clubs (7 iron, pitching wedge, and sand wedge). Repeat until you can get three to cluster together with each club.

228

Nine-Hole Challenge

Version 1—Select one hole as the target. Place balls at nine locations around the green. Chip to the hole and putt out from each location.

Version 2—Select one spot about 6 feet off the putting green. Chip and then putt out to **different** holes on the practice green.

Keep score and challenge teammates. A score of two is great, three is average, and four needs more practice.

PITCHING GAMES

Hula Hoop Toss

Place Hula Hoops 10 yards, 15 yards, 20 yards, and 25 yards from a starting point

Toss five balls underhanded and have them land in each hoop.

Now use your wedges (pitching wedge and sand wedge) to pitch five balls to each hoop.

FULL SWING DRILLS

Gate

Place two tees in the ground, with a slightly larger opening than the width of your golf club head, and center your ball between the two tees. Hit the ball without hitting either of the tees.

Swish Drill

Take your driver and grip the head of the club. Take full swings and create a swish sound. If there is no sound, your swing speed is too slow. Feel your weight shift from the back leg to the front leg.

Appendix #3

HOW TO SELECT A GOLF TEACHING

PROFESSIONAL

Appearance

Does he or she look the part? Yes, it does matter!

Lesson Schedule

Does he or she have a variety of options—private and group lessons?

Credentials

Does he or she have the education, certifications, and experience?

Communication

Is what he or she telling you making sense? A good instructor will be able to explain golf in simple terms that are meaningful to you.

Method of Teaching

Is there a 2D or 3D analysis of your swing? What about on-course options and playing lessons?

Personality

Do you like her or him? Are you comfortable with him or her?

Referrals

Talk with others who have worked with the instructor.

Appendix #4

GOLF BOOKS & MOVIES ABOUT THE SPIRIT

OF THE GAME

BOOKS

The Legend of Bagger Vance by Steven Pressfield

Golf in the Kingdom by Michael Murphy

Zen Golf: Mastering the Mental Game by Joseph Parent

Harvey Penick's Little Red Golf Book: Lessons and Teachings Learned from a Lifetime in Golf by Harvey Penick, Bud Shrake, and Davis Love III

The Greatest Game Ever Played by Mark Frost

Golf Is Not a Game of Perfect by Bob Rotella

MOVIES

The Legend of Bagger Vance

The Greatest Game Ever Played

Tin Cup

Caddyshack

Happy Gilmore

Appendix #5

ADDITIONAL RESOURCES

www.smashingballs.com

www.usga.org.

www.lpga.com

www.pga.com

Golf Magazine

Golf Digest Magazine

TV—The Golf Channel

www.smashingballs.com

www.activespinecenter.net

www.peggybriggs.com

Smashing Golf You Tube:

https://www.youtube.com/channel/UC86obUj0yrhqCez

g6dQO1bA

About Dr. Debra Pentz and Peggy Briggs

DR. DEBRA PENTZ started her work life as an accountant in the corporate world. After 15 years, she came to senses and made a dramatic career change. Actually her friends and family thought she was crazy to leave a well-paying secure job.

She attended Cleveland College of Chiropractic in Kansas City, and graduated as valedictorian.

A native of Pennsylvania, her love of golf and sunshine inspired her to move to Arizona where she opened a private chiropractic and physical therapy practice in Mesa, Arizona in 1999.

She has presented a series of workshops for Humana on golf fitness and injury prevention, and is a certified Titleist Performance Institute Fitness Professional. She is an active member of the Arizona and National Speakers Associations.

In the corporate world, Debra accidentally discovered the magic of golf as a business relationship builder. She learned that golf proved more valuable than a Master's degree in cultivating business relationships. She is excited about sharing this information to help women move into leadership positions that they so richly deserve.

She is co-founder of Smashing Balls Golfer Fitness and Smashing Balls Golf Adventures for Women.

In addition to golf, Debra loves wine tasting, traveling, hiking, fly fishing and kayaking.

~

PEGGY BRIGGS, LPGA STARTED playing golf later in her adult life. In spite of a late start she gained her Professional status in 1997, competing on the Players' West Mini-Tour. Prior to her golf career, Peggy was a flight attendant.

She enjoys coaching and training golfers of all levels. She is especially passionate about bringing women into the great game of golf. Peggy is an active member of the JGAA (Junior Golf Association of Arizona) and the AWGA (Arizona Women's Golf Association). She works with several local girls high school teams in the AWGA's Build a Team Program.

Peggy continually seeks knowledge to ensure that her students receive top quality instruction. She has added Titleist Performance Institute Certified Golf Fitness Instructor, 3-D Motion Capture using K-Vest Technology and Eye Line Putting to her credentials. Peggy taught 5 years with John Jacobs Golf Schools and utilizes methods learned from Manuel de la Torre Golf Seminars, Vision 54 Coaching Seminars and LPGA Golf Clinics for Women Instructors.

Peggy gives private and group lessons at Arizona Golf Resort in Mesa, AZ. She is co-founder of Smashing Balls

Golfer Fitness and Smashing Balls Golf Adventures for Women.

She's been married to her husband Jerry for 30 plus years. They enjoy flying, boating, hiking and golf.

Your Thoughts?

WE LOVE GETTING feedback from our readers and would really appreciate you taking a few minutes to post your comments or a brief review on our Amazon page.

Thank you!

Made in the USA
Columbia, SC
30 August 2018